RICK STEVES'
THE BALTICS
& RUSSIA

1996

Rick Steves and Ian Watson

John Muir Publications
Santa Fe, New Mexico

Other JMP travel guidebooks by Rick Steves:
Asia Through the Back Door (with Bob Effertz)
Europe Through the Back Door
Europe 101: History and Art for the Traveler
   (with Gene Openshaw)
Kidding Around Seattle
Mona Winks: Self-Guided Tours of Europe's Top Museums
   (with Gene Openshaw)
Rick Steves' Europe
Rick Steves' France, Belgium & the Netherlands (with Steve Smith)
Rick Steves' Germany, Austria & Switzerland
Rick Steves' Great Britain
Rick Steves' Italy
Rick Steves' Scandinavia
Rick Steves' Spain & Portugal
Rick Steves' Phrase Books for: French, German, Italian,
   Spanish/Portuguese, and French/German/Italian

Thanks to my hardworking team at Europe Through the Back Door; the many readers who shared tips and experiences from their travels; the many Europeans who make travel such a good living; and most of all, to my wife, Anne, for her support.

John Muir Publications, P.O. Box 613, Santa Fe, NM 87504
© 1996, 1994 Ian Watson
Maps © 1994 Rick Steves' Europe Through the Back Door, Inc.
Cover © 1996 by John Muir Publications
All rights reserved.

Printed in the United States of America
First printing January 1996

ISSN 1085-7230
ISBN 1-56261-276-X

Distributed to the book trade by
Publishers Group West
Emeryville, California

Editors Risa Laib, Rich Sorensen, Rick Steves
Editorial Support Dianna Delling, Nancy Gillan, Peggy Schaefer
Production Kathryn Lloyd-Strongin, Sarah Horowitz
Research Assistance Ellen Barry
Interior Maps Dave Hoerlein   **Cover Map** Kathryn Lloyd-Strongin
Typesetting Cowgirls Design
Cover Design Cowgirls Design, Kathryn Lloyd-Strongin
Interior Design Linda Braun
Cover Photo Rick Steves
Printer Banta Company

CONTENTS

HOW TO USE THIS BOOK

We wrote this book to fill several needs. There is very little written on independent budget travel in the Baltics and Russia, and most of what is available on this quickly developing region is out of date by the time it hits the bookshelf. The Baltics and Russia offer a world of travel thrills with plenty of hard-working local people eager to develop their entrepreneurial skills in this wide-open frontier of capitalism. They have a long way to go, and they could certainly use a few customers (with Western cash) to practice on. We hope this book will help give the local economies a much-needed boost by giving American travelers confidence, through fresh and clear information, to travel to the Baltics and Russia. We know the area is a great new travel destination. And it will never be more interesting than in 1996.

Our lean and mean format focuses only on the three Baltic capital cities and Russia's two most important stops. For the average first visit, these five cities are the predictable and best targets.

American newspapers give an over-gloomy impression of life in Russia and the Baltic states, focusing on crime, unemployment, fuel shortages, foul-temperedness, and ominous political events. In reality, for most locals, life goes on: People buy bread, go to work a bit, ride the subway, get married, dabble in business speculation, visit their grand-mothers, and grumble as much about the hardships of life now as they did about the "system" under Communism. Meanwhile, life gets better and better for tourists. Getting a visa, getting there, getting around, finding a place to stay, eating out, and meeting the locals are all markedly easier than they were even a year ago. Travel here also gives us "first-world" travelers a valuable opportunity to watch as circumstances force people to move away from an irresponsible system and toward one where they must responsibly marshal scarce resources to safeguard the health of society.

This book is organized into a flexible modular system. Each recommended "module," or destination, is covered as a mini-vacation on its own, filled with exciting sights, affordable places to stay, and hard opinions on how best to use your limited time. The chapter breakdown follows on the next page.

Planning Your Time, a suggested schedule with thoughts on how best to use your time.

Orientation, including transportation within a destination, tourist information, and a Dave Hoerlein map designed to make the text clear and your entry smooth.

Sights with ratings: ▲▲▲—Don't miss; ▲▲—Try hard to see; ▲—Worthwhile if you can make it; no rating—Worth knowing about.

Sleeping and **Eating** with addresses and phone numbers of my favorite budget hotels and restaurants.

Transportation Connections to nearby destinations by train, bus and boat.

Planning Your Trip

You can approach Russia and the Baltics from Scandinavia, Central Europe, or China. Helsinki is the best jumping-off point: You can get to Tallinn by hydrofoil in 2 hours, and to St. Petersburg by rail in less than 7 hours. From Warsaw you can take a 10-hour bus ride to Vilnius or a 22-hour train ride to Moscow. From Stockholm you can ride the overnight ferry to Tallinn. It may help to think of your trip as an excursion from Helsinki or Warsaw, or as an interesting way to connect Europe and Scandinavia. The Gateways chapter of this book has information on these routes. A final choice is to take the Trans-Siberian railway from Beijing to Moscow.

Those doing Europe with a rail pass can plan an "open-jaws" trip, using the pass in Western Europe first, finishing off with a Baltics swing, and flying home from any city featured in this book.

Two weeks is plenty of time to visit the five cities covered in this book. Moscow, St. Petersburg, and Tallinn are worth three days each; Riga and Vilnius can be seen in two. More than anywhere else in Europe, this region lends itself to overnight train rides. Whenever possible, connect towns as you sleep.

Figure out where you'll start and where you'll finish. If you're visiting only Russia, it's better to go from Helsinki than from Warsaw. If you're visiting only the Baltics, either will do. Of course, you can also fly from the U.S.A. into or out of any of the cities in this book (usually with one connection).

Whatever you do, plan to make just one pass through the Baltics, and one pass through Russia. This way you will have to get only one Baltic visa and one Russian visa. And if you have a choice, visit St. Petersburg before you go to Moscow. It's smaller, prettier, and can give you an idea whether you like Russia and really want to take the plunge and go to Moscow.

Itinerary Priorities

with 4 days:	Tallinn and St. Petersburg
7 days, add:	Moscow
9 days, add:	Riga
14 days, add:	Vilnius, and slow down

Major Transportation Connections

From	To (or vice versa)	Mode	Hours	US$
Helsinki	Tallinn	hydrofoil	2	$25
Helsinki	St. Petersburg	day train	7	$60
St. Petersburg	Moscow	night train	8	$33
Tallinn	St. Petersburg	night train	9	$20
Tallinn	Riga	night train	10	$15
Riga	Vilnius	night train	9	$16
Vilnius	Warsaw	day bus	10	$14
Warsaw	Moscow	night train	22	$74

Note: These fares were in effect in mid-1995; prices have increased since then.

Pack Along

Except for a few exceptions, pack for a trip to the Baltics and Russia as you would for a trip through Western Europe.

For Yourself: Consider bringing an emergency roll of toilet paper, a sink stopper, vitamins, and plastic bags (though you can get them on the spot, too) or a net bag.

For Gifts: These days you can get anything in the hard-currency stores, so the best sure-fire pleaser is Western cash. Top quality, duty-free candy and chocolate, always easy to get on the ferry from Scandinavia, are much appreciated. Postcards, stickers, pins, T-shirts, hats, and decals from the U.S.A. (the more Western-looking the better), well-chosen perfume or makeup, coffee, seeds (both vegetable and

Climate Chart

Average high/low temperatures (Fahrenheit) and average rainy days per month

City	Jan	Mar	May	July	Sept	Nov
Riga/	25°/14°	35°/20°	61°/42°	71°/52°	63°/47°	39°/30°
Vilnius	19	16	13	12	17	19
St.	19°/8°	32°/18°	59°/42°	70°/55°	60°/47°	35°/28°
Petersburg	21	14	13	13	17	18
Moscow	15°/3°	32°/18°	66°/46°	73°/55°	61°/45°	35°/26°
	18	15	13	15	13	15
Helsinki/	26°/17°	32°/20°	56°/40°	71°/55°	59°/46°	37°/30°
Tallinn	20	14	12	14	15	19
Warsaw	32°/22°	42°/28°	67°/48°	75°/58°	66°/49°	42°/33°
	15	11	11	16	12	12

flower), tapes, and Western-printed Russian–English dictionaries are also good gifts.

When to Go
Summers are cool in the Baltics and Russia. Some days will be warm enough to wear just a T-shirt, but definitely pack a sweater for the evenings. Summers in Moscow bring thunderstorms like clockwork late in the afternoon. Don't trust the blue sky when you wake up; bring that umbrella. Winters are dark, cold, and dreary.

Recommended Guidebooks and Maps
This book is one of a series of eight Rick Steves' country guides. If you wish this book also covered Helsinki, Stockholm, and Copenhagen, *Rick Steves' Scandinavia* (Santa Fe, N.M.: John Muir Publications, 1996) is the guidebook for you.

Let's Go: Eastern Europe 1996—Written by students, geared for young backpackers, this book covers 17 countries, including the Baltics and western Russia. Your *Rick Steves' Baltics & Russia* co-author Ian Watson is a former editor of *Let's Go: Europe.*

Lonely Planet's *Russia, Ukraine, and Belarus* (1996) and *Baltic States and Kaliningrad* (1994) are good sources if you want more information on these regions, especially outside of the capital cities.

The Insight Guide: Baltic States has informative essays and good photographs, but it's a little heavy to carry. *The Baltic Revolution*, by journalist Anatol Lieven, is currently everyone's favorite book on modern Baltic history, politics, and society.

Local English-language newspapers such as the *Baltic Independent* (based in Tallinn), the *Baltic Observer* (based in Riga), the *Moscow Times*, and the *St. Petersburg Press* are a great source for the latest news, and also carry entertainment schedules. And once you're in St. Petersburg you'll find a wonderful, locally produced, English-language guidebook to St. Petersburg published by Fresh Air Publications.

Maps of the Baltic capitals are easy to get. However, it's worth picking up maps of Moscow and St. Petersburg in the West (try to get a recent map with street names in both Cyrillic and Roman) since there are periodic shortages in Russia.

Transportation in the Baltics and Russia

By Train

The beauty of the region is that each of the five cities in this book is an easy 8- to 16-hour overnight train ride from each of the others. Overnight trains are an institution in Russia and the Baltics. The scenery between cities is nothing to lose sleep over. You'll board sometime in the evening, perhaps after an early dinner. Bring a late-night snack, a banana for breakfast, and enough to drink. Car doors open 20–30 minutes before departure. Armed with your train number, locate your platform on the announcement board in the station and show your ticket to the conductor as you step onto your car. She'll return as soon as you get underway to collect your ticket (giving it back before you arrive), to demand the local equivalent of 50 cents or so for your clean sheets, and (in luxury compartments) to bring you tea on request. A few hours later, the lights go out, and you can sleep—until you hit the border and the customs guards knock on your door.

Soviet sleeper compartments were, and are, among the nicest in Europe. Available only on better trains, two-bed, first-class compartments called *lyuks* or CB are an affordable luxury. Four-bed, second-class *kupe* compartments are still much roomier than Western Europe's six-bunk couchettes. Groups of three will find the trip more pleasant if they buy out an entire four-person *kupe* compartment.

Transportation Connections

Departures from each city are listed in the respective chapter, and although new schedules come out annually at the end of May, year-to-year changes are minor. Still, be sure to confirm times at the station. Prices, on the other hand, are going up every month, so use the listed ones as approximations. Times are all local. Trains usually run on time. Note that in the ex-U.S.S.R., express trains carry people almost exclusively from the first station to the last (in other words, almost everyone on a Moscow–St. Petersburg train got on at Moscow and will get off in St. Petersburg).

Your biggest hassle will be buying tickets. The hallmark of the system is that there are separate windows for local, for national, and for international trains, and for

Deciphering Your Train Ticket

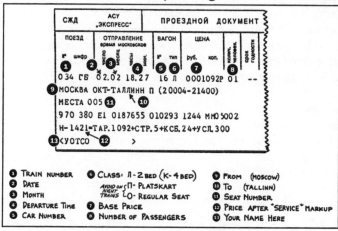

advance and for same-day tickets. In Tallinn and Riga, all of these are fortunately grouped at the train station, or *vokzal*. In Vilnius, St. Petersburg, and Moscow, however, these "windows" are spread out among several different offices all over the city. And in Russia, there's an added complication: Foreigners can only buy train tickets at the special windows for foreigners—although the clerks there generally speak no language but Russian, and the tickets are the same as Russians get but more expensive. In each city chapter, we've described the intricacies of the local system and possible solutions.

Note that prices and policies differ from city to city, even for the same tickets on the same train. For example, you can buy a round-trip Tallinn–Moscow–Tallinn ticket in Tallinn, but not a Moscow–Tallinn–Moscow ticket in Moscow. What's more, a Moscow–Tallinn ticket bought in Tallinn costs less than in Moscow.

Especially in Russia, keep hassles to a minimum by handing the clerk a sheet of paper (see sample in Appendix) with your destination, date of travel, preferred train number or departure time, the number of seats you want, your desired class (write a K for four-bed *kupes*, or SV for luxury two-bed compartments), and your last name. Cheaper tickets for P, O, or S classes are available on virtually any train. Especially on long journeys such as overnight trains, avoid these cheaper classes unless you enjoy hard, non-reclining seats. The word for train station in Russia is Вокзал (pronounced "voksal," same as in the Baltics).

When you get your ticket, you may have trouble deciphering it. We've included a sample train ticket in this chapter for easy reference.

By Bus
Buses are useful between Tallinn, Riga, Vilnius, and Warsaw, and between St. Petersburg and Helsinki. Ticket buying is generally simpler, with no distinction between foreigners and locals, and no need to show up as far in advance.

Within Cities
Try to walk. The only place where you absolutely have to take public transportation is Moscow. In every city you can buy single bus tickets (punch them on board) from kiosks and Metro tokens from booths inside the entrances. Or, for a few dollars, you can buy a card good for unlimited public transportation for one calendar month.

Taxis are still fairly cheap, but the only city where drivers usually use the meter is Tallinn. You'll have to haggle, or else keep silent about the fare until the end and then refuse to pay more than a fair price. Don't expect official drivers all the time; private citizens may pick you up too, and this is considered normal. Don't be shy about refusing a ride if you don't trust the driver or if he asks too much money. A ride around the center of town should not cost more than the local equivalent of $2. Rides out to the suburbs shouldn't be more than $3–$4. Pay in local currency.

Arriving and departing from airports, you will always find it cheaper to take the bus into the center of town. If you must take a taxi, prepare to get ripped off. Even if you take the bus into town and then a taxi, you'll have a better chance of getting an honest deal.

Sleeping in the Baltics and Russia
While costs are generally cheap in this region, finding budget accommodations can be more of a problem. To get Western comfort you'll often have to pay Western prices. Most decent hotels cater to business travelers or have a special pricing system

that enables locals to sleep affordably but soaks Western travelers. This is starting to change, and each city has a few budget alternatives (as explained in each chapter).

Considering how big these cities are, accommodations are few and far between. Considering how many tourists visit them, it's about right. Places of particularly good value are very difficult to find without listings such as those in this book. And because traveling in this region is more complicated than in Western Europe, your hotel is as important as a local agent for information, tickets, and visa needs as it is for its bed and shower.

Things are much easier for the budget traveler now than in the 1980s. Youth hostels and bed-and-breakfast networks are particularly handy for budget independent travelers of any age. But be warned, budget travel does not insulate you from the everyday struggles of the local people. For instance, many municipal hot-water heating systems shut down for maintenance for a few weeks each summer, and entire towns (except for the very expensive hotels) go without hot water.

Eating in the Baltics and Russia

Few of the new, service-oriented restaurants that have sprung up lately serve Russian or Baltic food. Most of the restaurants listed in this book serve Chinese, Italian, Indian, American, or vaguely international food. Russian and Baltic cooking emerged from Communism ravaged and mutant. Much of what was considered best about Russian cuisine during the Communist period actually came from more abundant areas of the Soviet Union such as Central Asia and the Caucasus.

Truly local cooking relies on bread, meat, potatoes, berries, sour cream, and northern vegetables such as cabbage, carrots, and beets, topped off with fruit compote, tea, cakes, and vodka. The best way to experience an authentic meal is on the rickety living room table in a new friend's apartment. Russians and Balts themselves almost never go out to eat, but they love having guests for dinner. Though tasty enough, local food is often a disaster cocktail of salt, fat, and sour cream, which together with industrial pollution and poor standards of exercise, sanitation, health education, and hygiene, has corrupted the well-being of millions of people across the former Soviet Union. Amid this desolation, foreign cuisine often holds out the only hope of nutritional salvation. In Moscow, going to McDonald's can actually feel like a square meal.

Restaurants

Despite rising prices, you can eat a satisfying restaurant meal in any of these cities for $5–$10 a person. Most establishments will add a service charge of 5 percent to 20 percent to the bill. You can then pay the exact amount, although it is common to round things up.

Finding good restaurants, particularly in Russia, is the big problem. It is still possible to stand in a long line and pay pennies' worth of rubles to eat gagging, lukewarm food at stand-up tables in a dimly lit, filthy café with puddles of tracked-in rainwater on the floor. And it's easy to eat mediocre $20 meals at proudly exclusive restaurants with offensive doormen, sleazy variety shows, thick-walleted customers with dark glasses, and waiters who pretend it's absolutely natural to pay 20 bucks for dinner in this part of the world.

In the Baltics you can easily find good meals for $5–$10. In Russia budget options are limited to pizza, fast food, and a few ethnic restaurants. For the best value, use the listings in this guidebook and the advice of your hotel or hostel manager.

When in search of a bathroom in a restaurant, remember: A downward-pointing triangle means "men," an upward-pointing triangle means "women." (Think "missionary position.")

Picnics

Picnics are a fine option. Bread is best bought from state stores, which you should visit at least once to experience the long lines and the Byzantine payment system. Find the price of whatever you're buying, go over to a cashier to pay that amount and get a receipt, and then present the receipt at the bread counter. Look for the dark, heavy brown loaves which Russians call black bread. Say *chorny* (чёрный) and they'll understand what you want. Next, head for a farmer's market for the best selection of cheese, sausage, and fresh fruits and vegetables. For Western staples like peanut butter, raspberry yogurt, or Cadbury chocolate, head to one of the many grocery stores that sell imported goods.

Water

If you want to stay absolutely on the safe side, drink only boiled or filtered water, soft drinks, tea, and juice in Russia and the Baltics. This is especially true in St. Petersburg, where a parasite called giardia infests the water system. It causes stomach upset and diarrhea, but can be eradicated with a prescription drug called *Flagyl* (metronidazole). Most visitors to St. Petersburg don't get sick, and if you avoid unboiled St. Petersburg water you should be okay, too. I brush my teeth with St. Petersburg water and just don't swallow.

Safety and Health

Despite the recent vast increase in crime, Russia and the Baltics are still far safer than New York. Crime here is coarser, cruder, and less professional than in America, often just a fight picked on the street or the drunken thuggery of unemployed young men. The Russian Mafia is interested in businesses and longterm residents, not tourists. Gypsy children can be a problem, especially at train stations.

Use the same precautions you would at home or anywhere else in Europe: Don't flaunt wealth, keep valuables in your money belt, avoid dark alleys, and don't talk back to drunks. Don't speak English loudly in public, and try not to draw attention to your foreignness.

Trains are generally safe, but it's wise to take some simple precautions. It's getting expensive to buy out an entire train compartment, but women traveling by train may be able to ask the conductor for permission to switch seats into a compartment with other women. You can lock the compartment door with the metal flip lock. For extra security, stuff a wad of paper, a cork, or a cut-off film canister into the cavity of the flip lock so that it can't be jimmied from the outside. Some people even tie down the door handle with a length of cord.

Ultimately, you are more at risk from dilapidation and decay—falling glass, open manholes, and the like—than from criminals. This is fortunate, since the local police are not renowned for their quick response or helpfulness. (Emergency numbers in Russia and the Baltics are: 01 for fire, 02 for the police, 03 for an ambulance.)

As for health, elementary precautions are in order, but paranoia is unnecessary. Watch what you eat and drink. Don't drink the water. Avoid dubious meat and be careful about eating street food. Make sure your shots are up to date. If you're going to be in Eastern Europe for a few months, it might be worth getting a gamma globulin shot to guard against hepatitis. Get advice from your doctor. Take a basic first-aid kit and any special medicines you may need. Distrust local hospitals; if you have serious problems, consult your embassy for a referral to a Western doctor, or head for Finland.

Money, Banking, and Exchange Rates

It's possible to change money at currency exchange desks in Russia and the Baltics at almost any time of day. You should avoid changing at "mini-market"-type kiosks or with wad-wavers on the street.

Estonia, Latvia, and Lithuania have fairly stable, permanent currencies: the kroon, the lat, and the litas. In Russia, the ruble's value varies considerably from day to day, so many prices are listed in dollars and then converted into rubles at that day's exchange rate. In this book, too, all Russian prices are listed in dollars, but you will always pay in rubles. Although dollars do circulate as an unofficial currency in Russia, you should politely refuse if taxi drivers or kiosk owners ask you to pay in dollars.

It's now possible to exchange American Express traveler's checks in all five cities in this book. In Tallinn, most banks will accept traveler's checks with a minimal commission. In Riga, Vilnius, St. Petersburg, and particularly Moscow, fewer banks take traveler's checks, and commissions are stiffer. If you bring traveler's checks at all, don't bring

---

August 1995 Exchange Rates

One U.S. dollar = approximately . . .

11 Estonian kroons	4 Lithuanian litas
0.5 Latvian lats	2.4 Polish zlotys
4,400 Russian rubles	7 Swedish kronor
4.4 Finnish marks	

more than half your money in them. U.S. cash dollars are better, and you can carry them safely in a neck pouch or money belt (call us at 206/771-8303 for a free catalog/ newsletter). Bring only new or nearly new currency. Worn, inky, heavily creased, or pre-1990 dollars are frequently not accepted in Russia. Carry smaller bills—twenties, tens, and plenty of fives and ones—since people who deal with hard currency often don't have exact change.

Business Hours and Red Tape

In Russia and the Baltics—and in this book—you'll be using the 24-hour clock. After 12:00 noon, keep going: 13:00, 14:00, etc. For anything over 12, subtract 12 and add p.m. (for example, 15:00 is 3:00 p.m.).

It's common for Russian shops to open on Sundays—the legacy of atheism. In the Baltics, fewer stores are open on Sundays. Especially in Russia and at state-run shops, there's an hour-long break for lunch, either 13:00-14:00 or 14:00-15:00.

The three-line system: At many stores in Russia and the Baltics you must stand in three lines: first, at the counter, to decide what you want and total up the price; second, to pay the cashier and get a slip; and third, to present the slip at the counter and get the goods. If you're buying food, you have to go through this once at the meat counter, once at the cheese counter, and so on. The Western system of selecting your own goods from the shelf and paying for them at one central location is catching on slowly. Supermarkets are a recent, welcome innovation.

Language

Latvian and Lithuanian are Baltic languages. Like Spanish and Italian, they are similar but not mutually intelligible. Russian is a Slavic language. The Slavic languages, the Baltic languages, and English all descend from Indo-European. Estonian, on the other hand, is a Finno-Ugric language, completely unrelated to the others. (Look at the words for one, two, and three in the Appendix word list; the similarities and differences jump right out.) Estonian is a lot like Finnish with the last letter of every word cut off.

Many young people in the Baltics and Russia have stud- ied English and can communicate basic phrases. Particularly in Estonia, most young people speak enough to deal with basic service questions. In Estonia and Latvia, many people over 60 speak some German. Just about everyone in the Baltic states speaks Russian. Sensationalists warn that Balts will practically spit in your face if you speak Russian to them. This is only true of a tiny minority of militant nationalists. If you speak Russian, use it.

In addition to our favorite survival phrases, we've included the Cyrillic alphabet and some pronunciation tips in the Appendix. Those who make a point to memorize these things will travel smoother.

Mail and Telephones

The Baltic mail systems are now up to world standards. If you need to send a box home from Russia, for example, a good way to do it is to go to Tallinn for the weekend and send it surface mail from the main post office there. If you send a Christmas card from Russia, leave the year off.

Since the spring of 1993 the Baltic states have had their own country telephone codes. Estonia is 372, Latvia is 371, and Lithuania is 370. The city codes for Tallinn, Riga, and Vilnius are all 2. Certain special cellular and digital lines in Tallinn and Riga use different city codes, so watch out. The country code for Russia is still 7; the city code for Moscow is 095, for St. Petersburg 812.

The new 370, 371, and 372 codes are used only for dialing into the Baltics from outside the former Soviet Union. All calls within the Baltics and Russia are dialed as if the entire area were still part of the U.S.S.R. This means you dial 8 for long distance, then the old Soviet city code (Moscow 095, St. Petersburg 812, Tallinn 0142, Riga 0132, Vilnius 0122), then the local number. This is true no matter whether you call from the Baltics to Russia, Russia to the Baltics, from one Baltic state to another, or within Russia.

To make international calls from the Baltics and Russia, you dial 8, wait for a tone, and then dial 10 followed by the country code, area code, and local number.

Using the telephone in the Baltics and Russia is getting easier (and more expensive). Still, it often takes several tries to complete a long-distance call. You can make any kind of call from a private phone. If you don't have access to one, you can make local calls from any phone booth, local or long-distance calls from the colorful modern phone booths (that take phone cards), or either type of call from telephone offices in the center of each city. Since local calls are free from private phones, shops and offices will often allow you to make a quick local call if you ask politely.

AT&T offers USA Direct Service in Lithuania, Latvia, Estonia, and Moscow. These phone numbers are listed in the Appendix. Dial the local number (listed for the country you're calling from) to reach an English-speaking operator who will place your call to America. The bill awaiting you at home will run $2.50 for the service charge, $3.25 for the first minute, and $2.65 for each additional minute. USA Direct is convenient, but it's cheaper to dial direct from a public telephone office. Unless you enjoy squandering money, never use USA Direct to make calls within Europe, Russia, and the Baltics.

Surviving Russia

As conditions in the Baltic states diverge further and further from those in Russia, it becomes more difficult to write a unified introduction to the entire area. While travel in the Baltics is getting more similar every month to travel anywhere else in Europe, visiting Russia requires some special skills and special caveats.

Capitalists: Many new business people in Russia think that capitalism means "I now have the right to make lots of money, get a black Mercedes and slick clothes, and look down my nose at the sludge of everyday society." You can smell these folks a mile away. Do your best to encourage and patronize businesses whose idea of capitalism and freedom is, instead, rejoicing in the chance for anybody to work freely toward their own goals and dreams, charging fairly and with a smile and an open door, and thinking of the quality of society as well as the thickness of their wallets.

Food prices: Groceries cost much more in Russia than in the Baltics. Prices often meet and sometimes exceed those in America and Europe. And while Baltic food producers have regained their step after the shock of moving to the market, Russian food producers have been slow to react and have found it hard to compete with imports. The restaurant market is largely defined by Western businessmen, journalists, and government-funded consultants who are not paying their own bills, and a $10 meal is considered cheap.

Russian salaries, of course, have not kept pace with food prices, so how do people eat? Why aren't they starving—especially the elderly, subsisting on a monthly inflation-squeezed pension check, their savings soaked away by the ruble's swift decline? This can be hard to understand on a quick visit, since you're isolated from the channels that Russians use to get by. To start with, housing and transport are subsidized, so a larger percentage of one's salary can be spent on food. Many people do part- or full-time work that doesn't show up in official salary statistics, and get extra income from renting an extra apartment or selling a car. As for the elderly, most live with extended families. When their children are at work and their grandchildren at school, pensioners have the time to stand in line for the cheapest (albeit lowest-quality) groceries from state-run stores, or to find the very best bargains at the private farmer's markets. Many Russians are lucky enough to own or have access to a *dacha* (country home), where they spend warm weekends planting, picking, canning, and preserving fruit and vegetables to hoard through the long winters. These are their secrets of survival.

Squalor and disgust: Any guidebook writer faces a dilemma trying to describe Russia. On the one hand, he must discuss world-famous icons of culture and history, such as the Hermitage in St. Petersburg and the Kremlin in Moscow, with the reverence they deserve. On the other, he must expose the ugly and frustrating Russian life. A visit to St. Petersburg recently led a journalist for London's *Sunday Times* to remark that the country's "rudeness and illogicality . . . makes social life in such a place a horror only marginally preferable to burning for eternity in hell."

That is an extreme statement, but almost every Westerner in Russia feels this way sometimes. Moscow *is* one of the great cities of the world—but as such it has more in common with Beijing and Mexico City than with New York and Paris. By Western standards, Russia first disappoints, then maddens, and finally saddens. It is racked by ecological devastation and economic hopelessness. Life in Moscow and

St. Petersburg is as expensive as the West and as squalid as much of the Third World, and the weather, scenery, and cuisine are better elsewhere.

Then why visit? Well, Russia is, in places, breathtakingly lovely. In other places, it is awesome. (Standing in front of the Stalin-era skyscrapers in Moscow, one cannot help but feel both fear and respect.) And though public life on the streets in Russia is very difficult, individual people, especially inside their own apartments, are warm and giving. In museums, churches, and concert halls, Russia's cultural and artistic heritage survives.

And Russia is extremely important—to recent history, to the present, and to the future of the world. It is important to see and understand the evil that the Soviet system perpetrated on its people, in the same way as it is important to learn about the Holocaust. This is a country where millions of innocent people died under Communism, and where the state poisoned the lives of those who survived.

Although I have listed plenty of museums and typical sightseeing attractions in this book, it would be a great waste to visit Moscow and see only the "sights" such as St. Basil's and the Kremlin. Do see the sights, but also stand in line for train tickets, shop in state stores for a picnic lunch, and take the Metro during rush hour. You will get more out of your trip if you consider yourself not a tourist but a student and an explorer.

Yes, you must step through puddles, avoid open manholes, crowd onto escalators, search hard for a decent place to eat, and talk to many unfriendly people through tiny holes in large windows—but it's worth it.

Send Us a Postcard, Drop Us a Line

Although we do what we can to keep this book accurate and up-to-date, the Baltics and Russia refuse to stand still. If you enjoy a successful trip with the help of this book and would like to share your discoveries, please send your tips, recommendations, criticisms, witticisms, or corrections to Ian Watson and Rick Steves, Europe Through the Back Door, Box 2009, Edmonds, WA 98020. To share tips or get an update of this book before your trip, tap into our free computer bulletin board travel information service (on America

Online's Travel Forum). All correspondents will receive a two-year subscription to our Back Door Travel quarterly newsletter (it's free anyway).

Judging from the positive feedback and happy postcards we get from travelers using this book, it's safe to assume you're on your way to a great vacation—independent, inexpensive, and with the finesse of an experienced traveler. Thanks, and happy travels!

BACK DOOR TRAVEL PHILOSOPHY
As Taught in *Rick Steves' Europe Through the Back Door*

Travel is intensified living—maximum thrills per minute and one of the last great sources of legal adventure. Travel is freedom. It's recess, and we need it. Experiencing the real world requires catching it by surprise, going casual . . . "Through the Back Door."

Affording travel is a matter of priorities. (Make do with the old car.) You can travel—simple, safe, and comfortable—just about anywhere in the world for $60 a day plus transportation costs. In many ways, spending more money only builds a thicker wall between you and what you came to see. The world is a cultural carnival, and time after time, you'll find that its best acts are free and the best seats are the cheap ones.

A tight budget forces you to travel close to the ground, meeting and communicating with the people, not relying on service with a purchased smile. Never sacrifice sleep, nutrition, safety, or cleanliness in the name of budget. Simply enjoy the local-style alternatives to expensive hotels and restaurants.

Extroverts have more fun. If your trip is low on magic moments, kick yourself and make things happen. If you don't enjoy a place, maybe you don't know enough about it. Seek the truth. Recognize tourist traps. Give a culture the benefit of your open mind. See things as different, but not better or worse. Any culture has much to share.

Of course, travel, like the world, is a series of hills and valleys. Be fanatically positive and militantly optimistic. If something's not to your liking, change your liking. Travel is addicting. It can make you a happier American as well as a citizen of the world. Our Earth is home to nearly 6 billion equally important people. It's humbling to travel and find that people don't envy Americans. They like us, but with all due respect, they wouldn't trade passports.

Globe-trotting destroys ethnocentricity. It helps you understand and appreciate different cultures. Travel changes people. It broadens perspectives and teaches new ways to measure quality of life. Many travelers toss aside their hometown blinders. Their prized souvenirs are the strands of different cultures they decide to knit into their own character. The world is a cultural yarn shop. And Back Door travelers are weaving the ultimate tapestry. Come on, join in!

VISAS

Only a little of this chapter, which looks more intimidating than it is, applies to you, depending on which visa you need and where you want to get it. If you're going to Belarus, Poland, China, or Mongolia, you'll find visa information for those places elsewhere in the book.

Getting Your Baltic Visa

Americans need a visa for Latvia but can enter Estonia and Lithuania visa-free.

Get your Latvian visa in advance. This is easy now. Normal processing costs about $10. You usually pay double for same-day service (available in Helsinki and Stockholm, popular gateways to the Baltics). Bring your passport and a photo. Americans can get free visas at some consulates. Most Europeans need a visa to visit Estonia, and Canadians need visas for Lithuania and Latvia, but each Baltic state participates in a common visa system, so you never need more than one visa for the three Baltics.

In the U.S.A.

Latvia: Requires application, actual passport, one photo, $5, and a prepaid return envelope, allow up to ten business days; 4325 17th St. NW, Washington, DC 20011, tel. 202/726-8213, fax 202/726-6785. **Lithuania:** 2622 16th St. NW, Washington, DC 20009, tel. 202/234-5860, fax 202/328-0466. **Estonia:** 630 Fifth Ave. Suite 2415, New York, NY 10111, tel. 212/247-1450.

In Helsinki

All three Baltic consulates are within reasonable walking distance of the train station and Tallinn ferry terminals. **Latvia:** Monday–Friday 10:00–12:00, Armfeltintie 10, tel. 4764-7233. **Lithuania:** Monday–Thursday 9:30–12:30, Friday 10:00–12:00, Rauhankatu 13a, second floor; near Senate Square and the university; tel. 608 210, fax 608 220. **Estonia:** Monday–Friday 9:15–12:00 and 14:00–15:30, Kasarmikatu 28; take tram #10; tel. 622-0280.

In Stockholm
Latvia: Monday–Wednesday and Friday 10:00–12:00, Odingata 5, tel. 700-6305. **Lithuania:** Monday–Friday 9:00–12:00, Strandvägen 53, tel. 667 1134. **Estonia:** Storgatan 38, tel. 661 5810, Monday–Friday 10:00–13:00.

In Moscow
Latvia: Monday–Friday 10:00–12:00, ul. Chaplygina/Чаплыгина 3, Metro: Chistye Prudy/Чистые Пруды, tel. 923-6666. **Lithuania:** Monday–Friday 10:00–12:30, ul. Borisoglebsky/Борисоглебский per. 10, Metro: Arbatskaya/Арбатская, tel. 291-1501.

In St. Petersburg
Latvia: Monday–Friday 10:00–12:00, Galernaya/Галерная ul. 69, second floor; a few blocks down the Neva from the Admiralty; tel. 315-1774.

In Tallinn
Americans and others who require visas for Latvia or Lithuania but not for Estonia can get a Latvian or Lithuanian visa in Tallinn. Free same-day service (one photo required) is usually available from the **Latvian** embassy at Tõnismägi 10, room 110, tel. 681 670 (Monday–Friday 10:00–12:00) and the **Lithuanian** embassy at Vabaduse väljak 10a, sixth floor, tel. 448 917 (Monday–Friday 9:00–13:00 and 14:00–17:00).

Getting Your Russian Visa
Although Russia has loosened up quite a bit for foreign independent travelers, getting a visa is still an unavoidable pain which requires serious pre-trip planning. While these next paragraphs explain the routine, you can also go through the St. Petersburg youth hostel's Redondo Beach office (listed in next section)—they do it all for you.

A Russian visa is not a stamp in your passport, but rather a piece of colored paper folded into three sections. The first section is your entry (Вьезд) visa, which is torn off by the border guard as you enter the country. The middle section is blank-backed for registration stamps. The last section is your exit (Выезд) visa, which, together with the middle page, is taken away by the guard as you leave the country (leaving your passport with no Russian souvenir).

A normal single-entry visa is valid for one entry and one exit at any time between the dates listed on it. (Multiple-entry visas are available at an additional cost.) You can now travel almost anywhere in Russia on any kind of visa.

You'll be issued one of four main types of visas, depending upon your supporting documentation. For a **tourist** visa, you need a confirmation letter from the travel agency or hotel or hostel that you're using as a local contact, including the agency's Russian accreditation number. For a **business** visa, the most extendable type, you need an official stamped letter of invitation from a Russian organization— a company, a friend's company, or whatever. (The organization is supposed to be licensed for "foreign economic activities," but in practice—depending on the consulate— anything with an official-looking letterhead and stamp often works.) For a **private** visa, you need a notification slip (*izveshchenie*) which your Russian host gets from the municipal authorities. A **transit** visa is issued on presentation to the consulate or embassy of a train ticket through Russia, or in some cases into Russia (e.g., a Beijing–Moscow ticket). Tourist, business, and private visa support documentation needs to include your full name, citizenship, passport number, and birthdate.

With the proper supporting documentation, you can get your visa from any Russian consulate in the world. Try to go through the consulate in your home country, well before you leave. It's best to come in person, but you can do it by mail (call or fax the consulate for instructions). The application procedure is roughly similar all over the world, though every consulate has peculiar mutations. You will need three photographs, a completed application form (available from the consulate or many travel agencies), a photocopy of the front page of your passport, the visa fee (usually in cash or certified check), and one of the four types of visa support documentation.

Yes, the official-invitation requirement is absurd. Russia is the only country in Europe that keeps it in place for Western European and American visa-seekers.

Russian Sources for Invitation Letters

The Travellers Guest House in Moscow—The Guest House can help you with many different types of visas, they don't require that you stay there, and when you stop by in Moscow they will register you while you wait. For example, a one-month tourist-visa invitation letter costs $25, and can be extended to three months in Moscow. You will have to send or take the invitation letter to the Russian consulate yourself. See the Moscow chapter for more details.

The St. Petersburg International Hostel can provide tourist visas if you are planning to stay at the hostel during your trip, and can also provide business and multiple-entry visas if you need more flexibility with your stay. For tourists, nobody else in Russia is so able to combine a low per-night price with efficient visa support from American and European offices. Any of their agents will take your reservation and write you a tourist visa invitation that you can send or take to the consulate yourself, but their American office (tel. 310/618-2014) will even get your visa for you if you want. See the St. Petersburg chapter for more details.

Russian organizations—Just about any Russian organization can write a visa invitation for you, often claiming that you are coming to Russia for "business negotiations" (*peregovory*). So, for example, if a friend of yours works at an institute somewhere in Moscow, the institute could write an invitation for you. Make sure that the organization promises to register you when you arrive in Russia.

Getting Russian Visas from Travel Agencies

Nearly every travel agent in Helsinki and Tallinn seems to be "doing" Russian visas these days. They give full service; bring your passport and three photos and they will write your invitation and deal with the Russian consulate for you. Processing time ranges from three hours to ten days, depending on how much you want to pay (usually $40–$50 for the cheapest service, as much as $200 if you want your visa the same day). A major drawback is that you must physically be in Helsinki or Tallinn to apply for and receive your visa. And if they invited you, they have to register you. Quiz the agent closely about who is going to register your visa in Russia and how, when, and where they are going to do it; don't leave without a specific, reliable-sounding contact address in writing.

In **Helsinki**, try Russian Trade and Travel Oy (Vuorimiehenkatu 15, tel. 659 052, fax 659 053) or Merelle-Till Havs agency (Kluuvikatu 6, tel. 651 011).

In **Tallinn,** visit CDS Reisid, Raekoja plats 17, second floor, tel. 445 262, fax 313 666.

You may be able to get a visa through a travel agent in America or Europe by reserving one night's stay in an expensive hotel in Russia but asking them to write the visa for a longer period. This is a good option because the hotel will register you even if you stay only one night. I've heard but can't confirm reports that if you go to some Intourist offices in Europe and tell them you're staying with friends and just need an invitation letter, they will write one for about $30. Again, registration may be a problem. Don't let them tell you that "the person you're staying with has to register you."

Russian Consulates

In the U.S.A.

At all consulates, single-entry visas by mail cost from $40 (for service within 14 days) to $120 (for same-day service). Send an SASE (or use their fax-back service at 800/634-4296) and they'll send you an application form. Multiple-entry visas cost $140 and take three days.

The **New York** consulate, at 9 E. 91st St., New York, NY 10128 (Monday–Friday 9:30–12:30), has a useful information number, 212/348-0779, with an actually helpful recording giving complete details on the visa process. To talk to a real person, call 212/348-0926 (fax 831-9162). There are also consulates at **Washington, D.C.** (1825 Phelps Place NW, Washington, DC 20008, tel. 202/939-8903, fax 483-7579), **Seattle** (#2323 Westin Building, 2001 6th Ave. Seattle, WA 98121, tel. 206/728-1910, fax 728-1871), and **San Francisco** (2790 Green St., San Francisco, CA 94123, tel. 415/929-0862, fax 929-0306).

In Helsinki (4.4 marks = $1)

The Russian diplomatic complex in Helsinki occupies an entire city block next to the "Kaivopuisto" stop of trams 3B and 3T (if you're coming south on 3B, it's the stop after the last ferry terminal). You can also walk from the center of town. The consular entrance is at Vuorimiehenkatu 6 (tel. 661 449), near the corner of Ullankatu on the other side of the complex from the tram. By Russian standards it's extremely efficient, and even has an English-speaking window. In winter, or when crowds are light, applicants are even allowed to walk straight into the building, but sometimes you must line up outside the gate and be let in by a capricious guard (Monday–Friday 9:30–12:00, but get there at 9:00 for a good spot in line, particularly if you want a same-day visa; the sign that says the consulate opens at 10:00 is wrong). Two-day processing costs 50mk, next-day processing costs 200mk, same-day processing costs 300mk, and on top of this you pay a mysterious "fee" which depends on your nationality (84mk for Americans). Show them a Trans-Siberian ticket and they'll normally outfit you with a 10-day transit visa, which costs the same. Standard paperwork is required.

In the Baltics
It's possible to get a Russian visa at the Russian consulate in any of the Baltic capitals. In principle, it's even possible to get same-day service (for up to $100). But because of long lines, communication problems, and bureaucratic frustrations, it is not a first choice.

Registering Your Russian Visa
Russian visas state that "every person is required to register his passport within three days after his arrival in the destination point with the exception of holidays and days off." Those traveling on transit visas are exempted (you have no destination within Russia anyway). Registration consists of a stamp on the white page of your visa. Your host or inviting organization is responsible for bringing your passport and visa to be registered at one of Russia's most dreaded bureaucracies: OVIR (ОВИР), which rhymes with severe, and stands for the state Visa and Registration Authority. Foreigners are not allowed to deal with OVIR themselves, with one exception (see next section). OVIR permits some organizations, such as hotels, to have their

own stamps on the premises so they don't have to come to the office every day, and in fact any Russian hotel you stay in may stamp your visa even if they have no connection with your inviting organization.

Since restrictions on internal travel for foreigners were eliminated, registration has become an entirely pointless bureaucratic exercise. Without going into all the gory details, let's just say that the system is also too absurd and cumbersome to be perfectly comprehensible or perfectly enforceable. In practice, you should make sure that the organization that invited you registers you. You should try to have this done within three days of your arrival, although probably no one will care if you are late. Most important, make sure that your visa gets stamped at least once before you leave Russia. It matters little where. Leaving Russia with an unstamped visa is a fifty-fifty proposition. They might not notice; if they do notice, they might not care; if they do care, the border guards might only extort a $50–$200 "fine" from you, but they could prevent you from leaving the country.

Extending Your Russian Visa

If you have a business, tourist, or private visa, the only way to prolong your stay in Russia is to have your host or inviting organization apply to OVIR for an extension, a process which includes bringing your passport and writing an official letter using various stock phrases such as, "The matter will be dealt with according to the established protocol." You are not allowed to deal with OVIR yourself. Rules, fees, and extension lengths differ from one OVIR to the next and from one month to the next.

Transit-visa holders who need extensions are the only foreigners normally received at OVIR, since no organization is legally responsible for them. In **Moscow**, the city-wide OVIR office is actually called UVIR, and is located at ul. Pokrovka/Покровка 42, about a 15-minute walk from Metro: Kurskaya/Курская. Exit the station, take the tunnel across the main street, walk north (i.e., to the right), and ul. Porkrovka is several blocks up but the first major street. Turn left, passing a small movie theater on your right, and OVIR will be the green pastel building on your left just

before the Hotel Ural. Go in the front door, then in the door on your left, then wait in the line at door #1.
Extensions of 3–5 days are available without much hassle; for anything longer you must show them your outbound ticket. You will have to fill out an application, receive instructions on how to pay exactly 8,772 rubles into OVIR's account at any branch of the State Savings Bank (Сбербанк), go pay, and return the next working day to pick up your visa (Monday, Tuesday, and Thursday 10:00–13:00 and 15:00–18:00, and Friday 10:00–13:00 and 15:00–17:00, tel. 207-0113). In **St. Petersburg**, visit OVIR at ul. Saltykova-Shchedrina/ Салтыкова-Щедрина 4, at the corner of Liteinii Prospekt, near Metro: Chernyshevskaya/Чернышевская. Official hours for reception of foreign citizens are Monday 10:00–12:00, Wednesday 15:30–17:30, and Friday 15:00–17:00, but these could change or become irrelevant.

Leaving Russia with an expired visa is a major sin. Don't do it. While crossing the border at 2:00 a.m. on a visa that expired at midnight is likely to be overlooked, one or two days' lateness might get you "fined"; anything longer than that and you may simply not be let out of the country. If this happens, it is possible to obtain a special "exit visa" from OVIR. Ask for help from the organization that originally invited you. If all else fails, contact your consulate.

GATEWAYS TO THE BALTICS AND RUSSIA: HELSINKI, STOCKHOLM, AND WARSAW

Here are some tips to help you make it smoothly through the transportation and bureaucratic hoops you'll encounter if you use Helsinki, Stockholm, or Warsaw as a gateway to the Baltics and Russia.

Helsinki

Helsinki is a compact and convenient city, and an excellent gateway to the five cities in this book. The Russian Empire-era architecture and the Orthodox church in the center of town will prepare you for St. Petersburg. Pick up a free map when you arrive. For a rundown on sightseeing and budget sleeping, see Lonely Planet's *Scandinavian & Baltic Europe* or the Helsinki chapter in *Rick Steves' Scandinavia*.

Exchange Rate: 4.4 Finnish marks (mk) = $1

Telephone Code: Calling Helsinki within Finland, dial 90 before the local number. Calling from outside of Finland, dial the international access code of the country you're calling from, then 3580, then the local number.

Travel Agency: A handy travel agency specializing in ferry reservations out of Helsinki and Russian visas is **Atlas Cruising Center/Merelle-Till Havs** (Monday–Friday 9:00–17:00, Kluuvikatu 6, tel. 651 011).

Sleeping: Two places to stay in Helsinki are especially cheap and convenient for travelers to Russia and the Baltics. **Eurohostel**, a block from the Viking Line ferry terminal and about a 20-minute walk from the Baltic ferry terminals, is an upscale hostel with immaculate double and triple rooms (98mk–115mk per person) as well as singles without bath (160mk–175mk) and a free sauna every morning (Linnankatu 9, tel. 358/0/664 452, fax 655 044). They enjoy being helpful and are a great grapevine for the latest on travel to and through the Baltics. **Matkakoti Pilvilinna** is a guesthouse one block from the train station and about 15 minutes from the port (Vilhonkatu 6, tel. 630 260 or 607 072, fax 630 355). It looks like it should be in southern Europe, with a rough-hewn feel, creaky floors, and an old elevator in the center of the stairway. Its virtues are

convenience and variable luxury, from a 12-bed hostel-
style dorm room for 65mk per person to a bright double
with bath for 230mk–300mk. (Visa and MasterCard
accepted.)

Transportation Connections—Helsinki

By Train
Helsinki to St. Petersburg and Moscow: Taking the
train from Helsinki is a speedy option, since Finland uses
the wide Russian track gauge and the wheels don't have to
be changed. Helsinki's train station is right downtown,
within walking distance of most ferries. There is a separate counter for Russian trains at the end of the Helsinki
train station ticket hall (Monday–Friday 8:30–17:00,
Saturday–Sunday 9:00–17:00). They take advance reservations at tel. 0100-128 (dialed in Finland) and fax
358/0/707-2111, though these are not generally necessary
for the St. Petersburg trains. There are two trains a day to
St. Petersburg, and one to Moscow.

Trains Departing Helsinki

Destination	Leaves	Arrives	2nd class	1st class	Notes
St. Petersburg *Sibelius* (Pietari)	6:30	13:55	265 mk	431 mk	Finnish
St. Petersburg *Repin* (Pietari)	15:32	23:20	265 mk	491 mk	Russian
Moscow *Tolstoi* (Moskova)	17:08	9:15	506 mk	760 mk	Russian

Going to St. Petersburg, the Finnish morning train is
much nicer than the Russian afternoon train. The train from
Helsinki to Moscow is not a very good deal. You'll save 20
percent by going from Helsinki just to St. Petersburg and
buying a ticket from there to Moscow. And you'll save 50
percent by taking the ferry to Tallinn, and then the
Tallinn–Moscow night train.

Buses Departing Helsinki

Destination	Leaves	Arrives	Price	Students
St. Petersburg (Pietari)	7:15	16:05	230mk	207mk
St. Petersburg (Pietari)	9:00	18:15	230mk	167mk
St. Petersburg (Pietari)	12:00	20:50	197mk	177mk

By Bus
Helsinki to St. Petersburg: The Helsinki bus station is across Mannerheimintie from the post office and train station. Bookings for all buses can be made at the station or by phone (tel. 6136-8433, fax 6136-8426).

By Boat
Helsinki to St. Petersburg: The Baltic Line's M/S *Konstantin Simonov* cruises twice a week in season from Helsinki to St. Petersburg and back. The ship leaves Helsinki's Makasiiniterminaali on Mondays and Thursdays at 17:00, arriving in St. Petersburg the following morning at 9:30. It returns from St. Petersburg on Thursdays and Sundays at five minutes past midnight, arriving back in Helsinki on Thursdays and Sundays at 11:00. Bookings can be made through Atlas Cruising Center/Merrelle-Till Havs (see address above), or by phone at 9800-22584 in Finland, 358/0/651 011 from outside Finland. Most passengers take the entire four-day cruise, which requires no Russian visa (you sleep on board the ship), but tickets in the cheaper classes (from 175mk per person, meals included) sell out months in advance. You can also go one-way if you have your own visa.

Helsinki to Tallinn: During summer only, the fastest way to Tallinn is by **hydrofoil**, which takes 1½ to 2 hours. All hydrofoils leave from the Makasiiniterminaali. Hydrofoil service starts sometime in April (depending on how fast the ice melts) and runs until late fall. Both Tallink and Estonian New Line plan on having up to four hydrofoil trips per day (140mk, no student or youth discounts). The Tallink hydrofoils use the main Tallinn city harbor, within walking distance of the Old Town. The

Estonian New Line hydrofoils run to Pirita harbor in a suburb of Tallinn and provide free shuttle service to downtown. For tickets, contact Tallink in Helsinki at 694 808 or 2282 1211, fax 680 2475 (Monday–Friday 8:30–19:00, Saturday 9:00–14:00) and Estonian New Line at 680-2499 (Monday–Friday 8:00–16:30); you can also go to the port or visit almost any travel agent in town. Estonian New Line also runs an office at Fabianinkatu 12.

Ferries run year-round between Helsinki and Tallinn and normally take 3½–4 hours. Tallink does three or four runs a day from the new West terminal in the west harbor of Helsinki. Passenger tickets start at 100mk, cars cost 200mk.

By Air
If you're 25 or under, Finnair youth fares are a great deal. A one-way flight to Tallinn costs 235mk, to Riga 560mk, and to Moscow 775mk. Finnair also has some decent APEX fares, like a 1,255mk round-trip to Riga. The Helsinki airport buses leave regularly from the Finnair City Terminal Building next to the train station.

Transportation Connections—Stockholm

By Boat
Stockholm to Tallinn: Estline's new *Mare Balticum* replaced the M/S *Estonia* after the latter's tragic sinking in autumn 1994. It will connect Stockholm and Tallinn all year, running in one direction one day, and the other the next. Stockholm departures are at 17:30, arriving in Tallinn at 9:00 the next morning; Tallinn departures are at 19:00, arriving Stockholm at 9:30 (all times local; Stockholm is an hour earlier than Tallinn). Ticket prices are changing but start at about U.S. $75, higher on Friday and Saturday departures from either Stockholm or Tallinn. Students get about 25 percent off with an ISIC card. The cheapest berths start at 110kr for a place in a four-bed cabin; otherwise you sleep in an airplane seat all night. Round-trips cost twice the one-way fare, except on a special fare reservable only in Tallinn for Tallinn–Stockholm–Tallinn roundtrips for which you fix a return date that you cannot change. In Stockholm, reserve by calling 667-0001 (you can pick up the

tickets at the port). Free buses meet both arriving and departing passengers in Stockholm, connecting Estline's Tallinnterminalen at the Frihamnen harbor to Stockholm's Cityterminalen (central bus station, next to the train station). Buses to departing ferries leave Cityterminalen at 15:00, 15:20, 15:40, and 16:00.

The main problem for the traveler is to figure out which days the ferry leaves from Stockholm and which days from Tallinn. Note that a smaller cargo ferry called the M/S *Nord Neptunus* runs on the days the M/S *Mare Balticum* doesn't, and has space for 50 passengers. Tickets cost the same and it's an option if you absolutely must sail on a particular date, but it has no cabins (only an open room with bunks), runs an hour slower, and isn't met by connecting buses.

It costs about the same to take an overnight ferry from Stockholm to Helsinki, then another ferry or hydrofoil from Helsinki to Tallinn. You can take either Silja Line or Viking Line from Stockholm to Helsinki, but the Silja Line terminal is right next to the Tallinn ferry terminal in Helsinki. Although this route takes longer, it works smoothly every day, and the ships are a little more luxurious. Another advantage of this approach is that Eurailpass holders get a free or discounted trip to Helsinki.

Stockholm to St. Petersburg: On a Baltic Line ship you can sail overnight to St. Petersburg, see the city visa-free for a couple of days, sleep and eat on board, and return to Stockholm afterwards. There are two cruises a week from Nynashamm near Stockholm (free shuttle bus connects Nynashamm and Stockholm's central station, 1½ hrs). The five-day cruise leaves Nynashamm Sunday at 17:30 and returns Thursday at 17:00 (prices start at $440 per berth in two-berth cabins). The four-day cruise leaves Nynashamm Friday at noon and returns Monday at 16:00 (prices start at $190 in four-berth cabins). All meals are included. You also have to book at least one St. Petersburg excursion, which will cost at least $35, but you do not need a visa or any advance preparation other than booking ahead. One-ways are possible if you have your own visa. Call Baltic Line at 020/290 029 (from abroad 46/8/5206-6600), or stop by their office near Stockholm Central Station at Vasagatan 4 (Monday–Friday 9:00–18:00, Saturday 11:00–15:00).

By Air
Stockholm to Tallinn and Riga: If you're 24 or under, SAS and Finnair youth fares to Tallinn and Riga are a good deal (reservable up to 7 days in advance). SAS has one-way youth fares from Stockholm to Tallinn and Riga for $136. Estonian Air (tel. 233 666) has comparable youth fares on its daily flights to Tallinn.

Warsaw
Polish Visa: U.S. citizens do not need a visa for Poland. Canadians do. Getting a Polish visa is easy. You don't need an invitation and can get same-day or mail service from your country's Polish embassy. In **Vilnius,** the Polish consulate will issue you a visa in an hour or so at a cost of $25 for a regular visa, $14 for a 48-hour transit visa (Monday–Friday 9:00–13:00, Švitrigailos g. 6/15, at the corner of A. Vivulskio g., tel. 650 075). Canadians pay the U.S. equivalent of $50 and $25 Canadian. You need two photos. Similar conditions prevail at the Polish consulates in **Riga** (Elizabetes iela 2, tel. 321 617), **Tallinn** (Pärnu mnt. 8, tel. 440 609), **Helsinki** (Armas Lingrenintie 21, tel. 684-8090), **St. Petersburg** (5th Sovetskaya ul. 12/14, tel. 274-4318), or **Moscow** (Bolshoi Tishinskii per. 1, between Barrikadnaya and Belorusskaya Metro stations, tel. 254-3621).

Transportation Connections—Warsaw

By Train
Problem #1: Poland uses Western European track gauge whereas Russia and the Baltics (and Finland) use a wider gauge. *Problem #2:* The main line from Warsaw to Vilnius, the rest of the Baltics, and St. Petersburg cuts across a corner of Belarus on its way from Warsaw, so you need a either a Russian visa or Belarussian transit visa for this route. If you have only a Russian single-entry visa, overeager Belarussian border guards may tear off the first part of it, causing problems when you enter Russia after your trip through Belarus and the Baltics. *Solution #1:* They put new wheels on all the cars at the Polish border, but it makes a lot of noise. *Solution #2:* A prewar rail line directly across the Polish–Lithuanian border has been reopened. This means that you can go from Warsaw to the Lithuanian town of

Between Lithuania and Poland by Rail

Šeštokai (in Polish, "Szestokai") without cutting across Belarus, and thus without the extra hassle of a Belarussian or Russian visa. At Šeštokai you change to a Russian-gauge train which will take you further into the Baltics.

All the train tickets below are available from the international ticket windows (Kasy Międzynarodowe) on the top floor of Warsaw's Warszawa Centralna train station. At least one of the agents on duty usually speaks English.

Warsaw to Kaunas, Riga, and Tallinn via Šeštokai: A Polish train leaves Warszawa Centralna daily, terminating just across the Polish–Lithuanian border at Šeštokai, Lithuania. There you switch to the Estonian-run Baltic Express which connects Kaunas, Riga, and Tallinn. Second-class tickets to Riga cost $27, to Tallinn, $45.

Unfortunately, you cannot reserve a seat for the Polish portion of this trip; you may in fact want to catch the train at its originating station, Warszawa Zachodnia, in order to have a better pick of places.

Warsaw to Vilnius via Šeštokai and Kaunas: If you don't have a Belarussian visa (or if you don't want to risk losing part of your Russian visa), this is the only decent way to reach Vilnius from Warsaw by train. Take the overnight from Warszawa Centralna to Šeštokai, arriving early in the morning; after a layover in Šeštokai you can catch a mid-morning train which arrives in Kaunas two hours later and in Vilnius after lunch. Through tickets for the entire journey cost $21 in Warsaw; be sure to reserve a place in a six-person *couchette* compartment from Warsaw to Šeštokai (the best this train offers). Look into flying or taking the bus, which are more comfortable for the money. Trains going from Warsaw to Vilnius via Belarus require a Belarussian or Russian visa and are generally not worth the trouble.

Warsaw to Moscow: About half a dozen trains per day make the 22-hour run from Warsaw to Moscow, most on their way from Berlin, Prague, and the like. Try for a train that originates in Poland, as the cars will be cleaner and the conductors less sleepy when you board. The best of these is the *Polonez*, which leaves Warsaw every afternoon at 14:40 and arrives in Moscow the following day at 12:15. A second-class (three-bed) sleeping berth costs $52; a first-class (two-bed) berth costs $78. Some of the other trains only have Russian second-class (four-bed) compartments.

Warsaw to St. Petersburg: While there are two daily trains from Warsaw to St. Petersburg (the distance and cost are almost the same as to Moscow), these trains pass through Belarus, Lithuania, and Latvia on the way. Unless you have Belarussian and Latvian visas (and Lithuanian for Canadians), it makes more sense to fly, or to go first to Moscow and then later to St. Petersburg.

By Bus

Most buses out of Warsaw leave from Warszawa Zachodnia bus station. To reach it, take bus #127 west along al. Jerozolimskie from just outside Warszawa Centralna train station, and get off at the last stop. Buy tickets at the "Kasa Między-narodowa" window on the south end of the waiting hall. For most, this Warsaw–Vilnius bus option beats taking the train.

Warsaw to Vilnius: Three buses run from Warszawa Zachodnia to Vilnius, one leaving daily at 8:00 and arriving about 18:00, another leaving daily at 12:00 and arriving about 23:00. Tickets on these buses cost $13. There is also overnight service leaving at 20:30 and arriving the next morning; although the schedule board says this bus runs daily from Warszawa Zachodnia, information from Vilnius suggests that it actually runs three times a week from another station, Warszawa Wschodnia. Check ahead.

Warsaw to Riga and Tallinn: On Wednesdays and Sundays, an Estonian bus leaves Warszawa Zachodnia at 8:00, arriving in Riga at 21:50 that evening and Tallinn at 3:00 late that night. Tickets to Tallinn cost about $30.

By Air
Given the hassle involved in taking the train from Warsaw to the Baltics and Russia, plane fares are worth looking into. The Polish airline LOT has some excellent deals, for example $141 round-trip to Vilnius, $216 to Riga, $262 to St. Petersburg, and $278 to Moscow. The LOT ticket office is on the ground floor of the Marriott Hotel in Warsaw (Monday–Friday 8:00–20:00, Saturday 8:00–15:00, tel. 630-5009). In the U.S., reach LOT at 800/223-0593.

By Car
Do not cross the Polish–Lithuanian border by private car. The border at Lazdijai is unbelievably crowded. Waiting time can be up to several days. The Vilnius–Warsaw buses don't have to wait. We've heard that foreigners are also sometimes waved to the front of the line, but don't count on it. Obviously, hitching a cross-border ride with the locals is not a good idea.

Getting Your Belarussian Transit Visa
The Warsaw–Vilnius main line as well as the Moscow–Vilnius and Warsaw–Moscow trains go through Belarus. If you are traveling to or from Russia with a valid Russian visa, the Belarussian authorities will accept your Russian visa for transit across Belarus. This means that you do not need a Belarussian transit visa to go, for example, from Warsaw to Moscow, or from Moscow to Vilnius. Belarussian border guards can be a little capricious, so be secure in the knowledge that your Russian visa *does* work and don't let them tell you otherwise.

However, if you are traveling between Poland and Lithuania on the main Warsaw–Grodno–Vilnius line, you take a risk by traveling with only a single-entry Russian visa. The border guard may (or may not) tear off the first part of your visa. This could cause a problem when you try to enter Russia from the Baltics (after you've transited Belarus). For peace of mind, either avoid Belarus (easiest choice), get a Belarussian transit visa, or call the nearest Belarussian consulate for the latest information. Embassies in the U.S.A.: 1619 New Hampshire Ave. NW, Washington, DC 20009, tel. 202/986-1604 or 136 E. 67th St., New York, NY 10021, tel. 212/682-5392). Embassies in Warsaw (tel. 617-3212) and Vilnius (tel. 650 871) issue visas for $30 (same or next day).

MOSCOW, RUSSIA

Moscow encapsulates all that's good and all that's bad about Russia. Like the country, its vast size threatens to overwhelm you and swallow you up. You feel small under the press of its weighty buildings, starchy food, grime, and pollution. Among the sprawling tenement buildings and "Stalin Gothic" skyscrapers one can still find brilliant golden domes and reminders of Czarist days. But the Soviet penchant for gigantism forces the visitor to search out these glimpses of Russia's past like flowers in a field of tall grass.

Moscow lacks the inherent beauty of St. Petersburg, but visitors here will feel as though they are in a place where things are happening furiously. Some days Moscow will leave you mentally and physically exhausted, wondering why you decided to go there and when the plane is leaving. Other days, though, you almost like it.

The city is huge. Rides around the center can take an hour. And the contradictions that pervade its society take you on an emotional roller coaster. Russians will bump, shove, and yell at you in a bakery line, and then smile and offer you everything they have in their kitchen when you dine at their apartments. The cramped and crumbling apartments constructed by Brezhnev are so unattractive that even the simplest church seems incredibly beautiful. Moscow's nouveau riche streak around in their mud-splattered Mercedes and BMWs, while young mothers stand alongside *babushki* selling everything from a used pair of boots to a bottle of milk. For many Russians life is a game of survival and, during these times of awkward steps towards a market economy, the rules seem to change every day.

Russophiles are evenly split between those who prefer Moscow and those who would choose nowhere else but St. Petersburg. Regardless of how or whether it charms you, Moscow is an exciting city to visit.

Planning Your Time
Plan on at least two days in Moscow. For a good two-day visit, try the suggested schedule that follows.

Day 1

10:00 Arrive in Red Square by Metro, see St. Basil's, visit Lenin, and wander through the GUM department store.

13:00 Grab a quick lunch inside GUM.

14:00 Depending on the weather and your interests, head to the Izmailovskii Park flea market, the Tretyakov Gallery, Novodevichi cemetery and convent, or "any random Metro neighborhood" (explained under Sights, below).

18:00 Return to the center for dinner at Patio Pizza.

Day 2

10:00 Go back downtown and tour the Kremlin.

13:00 Get Georgian food at Guria or Iberia.

14:30 Spend the afternoon exploring downtown Moscow; stroll down the Arbat and then return to the center along the almost-parallel Novii Arbat. You can see the White House on the way.

18:00 Walk or take the Metro up to Café Margarita or the American Bar & Grill for dinner. If they're full, grab something more quickly at McDonald's, Kombi's, or Baku Liban.

Orientation
(tel. code: 7095; tel. code within Baltics and Russia: 8095)

Moscow is enormous, and daunting to the uninitiated. The city is organized in concentric circles. The outer ring road marks the city limits while most of the important sights are contained within the inner Garden Ring or the innermost Boulevard Ring. At the bull's-eye are the Kremlin and Red Square. The Moscow River cuts an arc through the center of the city, with its peak touching the Kremlin.

Tourist Information

There is an information desk at the Intourist Hotel but don't count on much help. Intourist runs efficient, reasonably priced, half-day tours from the Hotel Intourist on Tverskaya, near the Kremlin. If your tour includes Moscow University, you'll get a great panoramic view of the city.

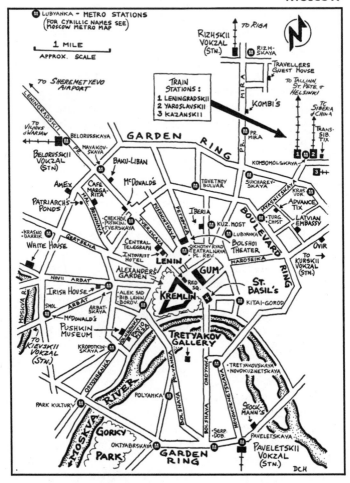

Currency Exchange

In Moscow it is easier to change money than to buy bread. Every neighborhood, often every block, sometimes every store has its own Обмен Валюты (currency exchange) desk, usually run by a bank. Little offices—even the exchange shacks inside shops—give better rates than desks in major hotels. A sizable number of banks now change traveler's checks, and at some establishments you can also pay with them, but it is still better to bring cash. A commission of 3 percent on traveler's checks is a good deal here.

One of the worst places in Moscow to change money is American Express. The Moscow branch provides the usual menu of services—including a 24-hour express cash machine dispensing traveler's checks—but at higher-than-usual commissions (3% on personal check cashing for card holders, 5% to change traveler's checks into dollars, and to make you feel even more downtrodden, security goons bar the door and let people in only one by one). If you lose your card or checks and have to go to AmEx, exit the Mayakovskaya/Маяковская Metro station and cross the street to the tower with the blue clock on it; then walk about 3 blocks along the Ring (Monday–Friday 9:00–17:00, Saturday 9:00–13:00, ul. Sadovaya-Kudrinskaya/Садовая-Кудринская 21a, tel. 956-9019).

Mail and Telephones

You can do everything at the **Central Telegraph Office**, ul. Tverskaya/Тверская 7 (Metro: Okhotnii Ryad/Охотный Ряд). The post office hall is on the right as you enter (daily

Moscow Metro

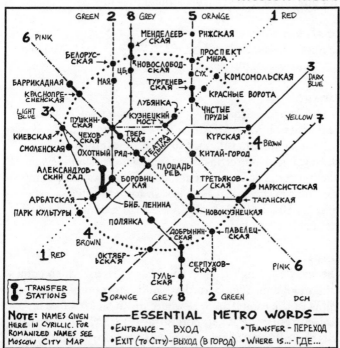

8:00–22:00). If you want to send a postcard, go to the window in the back left corner of the hall. It will take anywhere from a week to two months. If you actually want to communicate with someone, a better bet for value and speed is Global Sprint Fax. Go to window #13 on the left-hand side. You leave your document; they scan it and it's computer-sent; they notify you by phone if it fails to go through. One page to the U.S. costs $4, to most of Europe about $2.

For local calls you may use almost any public phone (there's no difference between a Таксофон and a Телефон). Most have been converted to take small plastic tokens, but some still require 1-ruble or 15-kopek coins—in all cases these are sold at kiosks for about 5 cents to 10 cents apiece.

For long-distance calls within the former U.S.S.R., you can go to the little room to the left in the vestibule of Central Telegraph (daily 7:00–22:00) or to any post office, but the best option is just to use a private phone. Rates are still low.

International calls are also easiest from a private phone, with direct dial now available around the clock.

American Embassy
Novinskii/Новинский bulvar 19/23, tel. 252-2451. Metro: Barrikadnaya/Баррикадная.

Bookstores
Zwemmers, at Kuznetskii Most/Кузнецкий мост 18 (near the Kuznetskii Most Metro station), has a moderate stock of art books and fiction shipped in from England, but doesn't sell travel guidebooks, maps, or anything printed in Russia. Like much of Moscow's retail industry it needs some competition, but meanwhile it's the best in town (Monday–Saturday 10:00–19:00, AmEx, Visa, MasterCard, and traveler's checks accepted).

News
The excellent English-language *Moscow Times*, which comes out Tuesday through Saturday, will keep you up-to-date on events in the capital and elsewhere in Russia. It's free at hard-currency stores and hotels. AM 918/FM 102.3 broadcasts the BBC in the mornings, and several other radio sta-

tions have news in English; check the Saturday *Moscow Times* for schedules.

Getting Around Moscow

Get used to the Metro. The stops (identifiable by a glowing red M) are never much more than a 10-minute walk away inside the Garden Ring road. If you do not see one, just ask any passerby "Gdye stantsiya Metro?" (or show them this: Где станция метро?) and you will likely be answered by *"Vot"* and an outstretched arm pointing the way.

Tokens for the Metro are available inside the entrances, though only a few at a time. The latest price should be posted near the ticket window. Go to the window, hold up the requisite number of fingers and say the number of tickets you want. For trams and buses you need to buy tickets which the drivers sell in strips of ten. They're also sold in and around Metro ticket windows. A unified month-pass (Единый Билет), available only the last and first few days of the month, costs around $20 and allows unlimited access to all modes of transportation.

Sights—Moscow

▲▲▲**Red Square, Lenin's Mausoleum, and St. Basil's Cathedral**—Any tour of Moscow should begin in the center of the city, on Red Square in front of St. Basil's Cathedral. Surrounded on one side by the Kremlin walls and Lenin's Mausoleum and on the other by GUM, the largest department store in the country, you'll rightly feel at the administrative heart of a grand empire. Though there is no longer any ceremonial changing of the guard in front of the mausoleum, you can go inside for free and decide for yourself whether Lenin is wax or flesh (Tuesday, Wednesday, Thursday, and Saturday from 10:00–13:00, and Sunday 10:00–14:00). Large bags and cameras must be checked in the cloakroom on the side of the maroon-colored, closed Historical Museum. Red Square's top ornament is St. Basil's Cathedral. Now more a plain museum with some old icons and a barren maze of rooms than a living church, its exterior is far more interesting than its interior. Even so, after you've given the outside a 360-degree marvel, peek inside.

▲▲GUM (ГУМ)—This is the best-stocked department store in Russia. Since 1992, hard-currency stores such as Benetton, Galeries Lafayette, and Samsonite have slowly begun to take over more and more space in GUM. There are three corridors; enter at either end. Climb up to the top floor at either end of the building where there are no stores and treat yourself to a spectacular view and an amazing vantage point for photographing ordinary Russians as they go about their shopping unawares. The natural light from the skylights is especially pretty on bright days. There's a fast-food chicken restaurant and a stand-up pizza joint inside. (Monday–Saturday 8:00–20:00.)

▲▲▲The Kremlin—The walled enclosure containing Russia's top government offices, as well as several beautiful Orthodox churches, is a must-see. The entrance is through Alexandrovskii Sad (Alexander's Garden); from Red Square, walk north past the mausoleum out of the square, go left into the garden and past the Tomb of the Unknown Soldier, and you'll come to the Kremlin ticket office, a small brown kiosk to the right of the white Kremlin rampart and across from the Alexandrovskii Sad/Александровский Сад Metro exit. You have to check your bags at the little office under the stairs.

The Kremlin is open Friday–Wednesday 10:00–17:00 (ticket office closes from 13:00–14:00 and at 16:30; closed Thursdays and during frequent official functions). Entry to the Kremlin grounds costs $0.15 for everyone. Entrance to each of the four churches is $6, students half-price, $0.15 for Russians. You don't have to see all four churches. Getting into the Armory costs $14, students half price, 60 cents for Russians. On summer mornings watch for newlywed brides and grooms who come to lay flowers at the Tomb of the Unknown Soldier back in Alexandrovskii Sad.

▲▲▲Izmailovskii Park weekend flea market—This is the place to buy your souvenirs. Most often you are dealing with the original artists, and bargaining is a must. Pick up a 13-piece *matryoshka* doll, beautifully hand-carved chess sets, or scarves and patchwork quilts. To get there, take the dark blue Metro line four stops northeast of the Ring line to Izmailovskii Park/Измайловский Парк—it's the station with a third track in the middle. Exit, turn left, and walk past the huge hotel toward the stadium and smokestacks in the distance. Notice the

Intourist propaganda posters on the right along the way. Open only on weekends and holidays, from morning till evening.

▲▲**The All-Russian Exhibition Center** (VDNKh/Вднх)— Once the Exhibit of the People's Economic Achievements, this center was a temple to the proletariat. Built in the 1930s, its 72 Neoclassical pavilions glorify Pig Husbandry, Standardization, Atomic Energy, and other giddy arts. Today it's hard to believe VDNKh was ever anything but a mall waiting to happen. Electronics is the name of the game, and every single structure has been transformed into a rabbit-hutch of cut-rate consumerism. Fascinating. (On Prospekt Mira opposite the Kosmos Hotel, concessions open 10:00–17:00, near Metro: VDNKh/Вднх).

▲▲**Any random Metro station**—To get a real feel for Russian life, try taking the Metro to any of the stations outside Moscow's Ring line. You can pick one at random, but here are some recommendations. For true Soviet residential bleakness it is hard to beat Yasenevo/Ясенево or Konkovo/Коньково, south on the orange line. If you prefer your bleakness dirty and industrial, head to the southeast, Moscow's most polluted region: Volgogradskii Prospekt/Волгоградский Проспект and Tekstilshchiki/Текстильщики on the pink line are representative stations. A more desirable neighborhood surrounds the Krylatskoe/Крылатское station at the end of the light blue line in the west of Moscow. Here the prevailing west winds are still unpolluted by the city's factories, and the 18-story tower blocks were built only recently. In another well-regarded neighborhood, around Sokol/Сокол to the north on the green line, you can see Stalin-era buildings from the forties and fifties.

In each case, check out the stores that Russians shop in as they walk from the Metro exit to their apartments after work each day. Since prices were liberalized, stores have been relatively well stocked. Aside from staples like milk and vegetables, many goods are imported. *Produkty* (Продукты) stores sell staples such as milk, sugar, and flour. A *bulochnaya* (Булочная) is a bakery selling bread, biscuits, and ginger-bread. *Moloko* (Молоко) stores sell dairy products. *Gastronom, Universam,* or *Dieta* stores combine all of the above under one roof. The local *univermag* (Универмаг) will probably be a much more representative department store than GUM.

Some neighborhoods now have a *supermarket* (Супермаркет)—a small, new store selling mostly imported food, where you check your bag at the door and then enjoy the wild freedom of shopping off open shelves.

Enjoy the Metro on your way. The most beautiful station is Mayakovskaya/Маяковская on the green line (don't miss the ceiling mosaics). Ploshchad Revolyutsii/Площадь Революции has arresting socialist-realist statues. The grandest stations are on the Ring line and the dark blue line.

▲**The Arbat** (Арбат)—If you're stuck in Moscow midweek and need to buy presents for friends back home, visit this pedestrianized street just west of downtown. Once a prestigious address for Russia's eminent writers, it not only retains some of its original grandeur but also has the best concentration of kitschy tourist shops in the city, graced by McDonald's at the far end. The closest Metro is the Arbatskaya/Арбатская station on the light blue line, directly across from the beginning of the Arbat—go through the underground passage full of middle-aged women selling puppies and kittens while artists offer to sketch you. The Arbatskaya station on the dark blue line is also convenient: exit, turn left, and walk through the crowds for about 250 meters. The Smolenskaya/Смоленская station on the dark blue line is at the Arbat's outer end.

▲**The White House** (Белый Дом)—If you want to see the scene of the October 1993 shelling (which finished the standoff between Boris Yeltsin and his hard-line foes in the Russian parliament), take the Metro to Krasnopresnenskaya/Краснопесненская on the Ring line and walk down the street past the red-brick new U.S. Embassy to the river. The White House has been repaired, as has the adjacent "municipal building" where the Duma now meets, but you may still see bullet holes in some of the fencework and guard-shacks near the municipal building. Security is tighter than it used to be but you should still be able to get a good look.

▲**Novodevichi Cemetery** (Новодевичье Кдадбище) **and Convent**—The walled convent, with its churches and graves, is one of the most peaceful places to escape to on a nice day in Moscow. Entrance to the grounds is usually free; if you want to see any of the museums inside you'll pay $1 each, Russians $0.30 (Wednesday–Monday 10:00–17:00). The cemetery, adjacent to the convent but with a separate entrance, contains the graves of Chekhov, Gogol, Bulgakov, Mayakovsky, Eisenstein, Shostakovich, Scriabin, Khrushchev, Molotov, Gromyko, and Stalin's wife, among others. It's one of the few major attractions in Moscow without a separate price for foreigners: entrance costs $0.50 for everyone, and the ticket office is across the street from the entrance (daily 10:00–18:00). Ask them for their English map ($0.30). To reach the complex, take the red line Metro two stops southeast of the Ring to Sportivnaya/ Спортивная, go out the exit towards the center, turn right and walk about 4 blocks along ul. 10-letiya Oktyabrya, and you'll see the spires of the convent across the street to your left. The cemetery is past the convent to your left.

▲**Gorky Park** (Парк Горкого)—Perhaps the best reason to go is the view from atop the enormous rickety Ferris wheel in the center of the 300-acre park. To get there, take the Metro to the Oktyabrskaya/Октябрьская Ring line station, exit to the street through the right-hand doors, go left around the corner, and walk alongside the park's fence about 400 meters to the huge colonnaded entrance (daily 10:00–22:30). Tickets are sold at the windows to the left and right for a few cents. Consider going back downtown on a riverboat, which you can catch at the terminal on the river side of the park.

▲**Tretyakov Gallery**—To get to the Tretyakov Gallery, which has the world's best collection of Russian icons and a selection of 18th- and 19th-century art (especially portraiture), take the orange line Metro to Tretyakovskaya/Третьяковская (don't go out through the connected Novokuznetskaya station, which will leave you several blocks away). Turn left at the top of the stairs, cross the street, and walk down the brick road about 100 meters to the large red and white building on the right ($6, students half price, Russians $0.30, Tuesday– Sunday 10:00–20:00, ticket windows close at 19:00).

▲**Pushkin Museum** (Музей Им. Пушкина)—This excellent fine-arts museum has roomfuls of paintings by Monet, Renoir, van Gogh, Rembrandt, and Picasso (Tuesday 10:00–21:00, Wednesday–Sunday 10:00–20:00, ul. Volkhonka/Волхонка 12, near Metro: Kropotkinskaya/ Кропоткинская).

▲**Sergiev Posad** (Сергиев Посад)—Formerly called Zagorsk, this is a living medieval monastery 60 km outside of

Moscow (Tuesday–Sunday 10:00–18:00). This world of onion domes and icons, one of the most beautiful churches in all Russia, is 90 minutes by local train from Moscow's Yaroslavskii Station (Metro: Komsomolskaya/Комсомольская). Coming out of the Metro, go in the glassed-in building under the large MOCKBA sign and buy an eight-zone *obratny* (return) ticket from any of the ticket windows (about $0.80), then hop on any of the trains marked Sergiev Posad or Aleksandrov (Александров), which leave every 10–30 minutes.

▲▲**Classical music or ballet**—Scout out posters and ask whoever you're staying with for advice on music, opera, and ballet performances. Getting into the Bolshoi Ballet usually requires paying scalpers these days (the going rate is about $10), but you can try at the ticket office across the square from the theater, next to the Teatralnaya/Театральная Metro entrance, between 12:00 and 15:00. It's always possible to hear great classical concerts for pennies at the Tchaikovskii Concert Hall at Metro: Mayakovskaya/Маяковская, or at the Tchaikovskii Conservatory on ul. Gertsena near Metro: Arbatskaya/Арбатская. Look in the *Moscow Times* for listings and stop by for tickets a day or so in advance.

Sleeping in Moscow
(tel. code: 7095; tel. code within Baltics and Russia: 8095; about 3,000 rubles = $1)
With the breakup of the state travel agency, Intourist, older hotels have "Westernized" themselves by raising their prices to Western levels without any change in the quality of the service. Newly built, Western-oriented hotels such the Slavjanskaya, the Marco Polo, the Aerostar, and the Palace are safe and clean but charge $250 a night . . . hard Western money only. Medium-priced hotels do exist, but they will not be able to help with your visa, may not speak English, and often don't take direct reservations from individuals.

The **Travellers Guest House** offers by far the best value—it's the only place to stay in Moscow which combines an affordable price with efficient, Western-oriented service. The guest house occupies one floor of a typical Soviet student dormitory, in which every two rooms share an entranceway and bathroom. A bed in a four-bed room costs $15, while a double costs $40 and a single goes for $30. Laundry service is available. The clientele is heavily American and British but the name "guest house" is appropriate, as the atmosphere is neither quite like a hostel nor like a hotel. Reserve early (Bolshaya Pereyaslavskaya/Большая Переяславская ul. 50, tenth floor, tel. 971-4059, fax 280-7686, e-mail tgh@glas.apc.org). From Metro: Prospekt Mira/Проспект мира, walk north about three blocks, turn right after the building with the red arch painted on it (you'll see four smokestacks in the distance), walk one block to the end of the street, turn left, and the guest house is in the tall white building on your right with red signs on either side of the door. Go in and take the elevator up to the tenth floor. The guest house is within long walking distance of the Rizhskii, Leningradskii, and Yaroslavskii stations and thus also of trains to Latvia, Estonia, and St. Petersburg as well as the Trans-Siberian.

The guest house takes bookings for the St. Petersburg International Hostel and also sells all sorts of train tickets (e.g., to St. Petersburg, Europe, and China). Their markups range from zero to modest, and they will sell tickets to non-guests. See the end of this book for more information on their Trans-Siberian packages.

The Travellers Guest House can also fax you visa support documentation—in other words, an invitation letter which you submit to the consulate to get your visa—regardless of whether or not you plan to stay there. When you arrive, they will register you while you wait. The cheapest invitation, for a one-month tourist visa extendable to three months, costs $30. A one-month business visa invitation costs $45, a six-month, three-entry business visa invitation goes for $125 and takes two weeks to process, and a one-year multi-entry visa invitation costs $250. Contact them from anywhere in the world by fax or e-mail with your full name, citizenship, passport number, birthdate, and city where you plan to apply for the visa. They normally ask for prepayment by credit card.

The **Prakash Guesthouse**, run by an Indian expatriate, offers 28 singles and doubles (starting at $20, includes private bath), along with Indian and Continental cuisine and nightly Indian movies. It's located 20 minutes from the Kremlin by Metro, right next to Metro: Belyayevo/Беляево (exit metro and turn toward the city, guesthouse is in first big building on your right, ul. Profsoyuznaya/Профсоюзная

83, Korpus 1, Entrance 2, visa support services available, tel./fax 334-2598).

The **Gostinitsa Izmailova**, a major Soviet hotel, is a distant third choice. If you can ignore the thriving sex industry in the lobby, you'll find fairly cheap rooms: singles start at $30, doubles at $45. This monolith is right next to Metro: Izmailvskii Park/Измайловский Парк and the weekend flea market (Izmailovskoe/Пзмайловское shosse 71, call ahead, tel. 166-3627).

Eating in Moscow

The first thing that should be said about restaurants in Moscow is that you will find few average locals at them, as the prices are prohibitive to all but the wealthiest. Most Muscovites dine outside their homes only at weddings. Secondly, restaurant character changes frequently. The clientele has a way of quickly transforming from clean-cut youth to *mafiosi*, and quality often lapses over time. A restaurant that serves good food cheaply and does so over a period of years is rare. Here are the latest best values:

McDonald's (МакДоналдс)—The golden arches attract Muscovites and foreigners alike with cleanliness, efficiency, relatively cheap prices, and predictably edible food. Indeed, this is the place to go when a quick lunch must be squeezed into a full day's sightseeing or when dinner plans fall through. Moscow's oldest and biggest McDonald's is at Metro: Pushkinskaya/Пушкинская, directly across from the statue of Russia's beloved national poet, Aleksandr Pushkin. In the best tradition of Soviet gigantism and American capitalism, Mickey D's boasts 27 cash registers, 1,500 employees with beaming smiles, seating for over 700, and nearly 40,000 customers a day. It even has its own farm to ensure an adequate supply of all the sesame seeds and special sauce required to make the Big Mac you try here taste like the one you last ate back in the States. There are sometimes lines, but they move fast. The other big McDonald's in Moscow is at the outer end of the Arbat, behind Metro: Smolenskaya/Смоленская. It is sometimes less crowded, and the upstairs room is a nicer place to sit and linger. Check out the great bakery two blocks away at Smolenskaya/Смоленская 6. There is a third, small McDonald's across from Central

Telegraph on ul. Ogareva/Огарева, a side street just off Tverskaya, near Metro: Okhotnii Ryad/Охотный Ряд, but it has only a few seats. At each location, a Big Mac, large Coke, and large fries cost about $3.60 total (Monday–Friday 9:00–23:00, Saturday–Sunday 10:00–23:00).

Kombi's (Комби'с) is Moscow's closest thing to a Western sub shop, selling sandwiches for $4–$5 and their trademark Oreo milkshakes for $1.50. They have an English menu. There are several locations in Moscow, all open daily from 10:00 to 22:00. One is a short walk from Red Square at ul. Tverskaya/Тверская 4, across the street from the Hotel Intourist near Metro: Okhotnii Ryad/Охотный Ряд, and another is at ul. Tverskaya 32, across the street from the exit at Metro: Mayakovskaya/Маяковская (go left at the top of the escalators). The original Kombi's is at Metro: Prospekt Mira/Проспект Мира; go out the Ring line exit so you don't have to cross the street, then walk a block up to Prospekt Mira 48. This is extremely convenient for people staying at the Travellers Guest House. Next door to this Kombi's is the Chicken House restaurant (daily 12:30–23:30), which will serve you a half-chicken for $8 and salads for $3–$5.

Baku Liban (Баку Либан)—For a place frequented by locals, try this stand-up Lebanese restaurant (daily 10:00–22:00, ul. Tverskaya/Тверская 24). Dine on sandwiches of shaved beef and chicken prepared in front of you (about $1 each) or falafel ($0.75). They also have hamburgers and more traditional rice and potato dishes. For dessert try a honey-drenched *makaron* (макарон) or *mshabbak* (мшаббак) pastry ($0.35). If language is a barrier, just point to what you want. The well-signposted restaurant is along the east side of Tverskaya halfway between the Mayakovskaya/Маяковская and Tverskaya/Тверская stations on the green line, next to the Hotel Minsk. Go in the poorly marked door on the right; the one on the left leads to the expensive sit-down section.

Georgian food—If you have never tried Georgian cuisine, Moscow is a good place to do it. It's an easy choice for vegetarians especially. There are two manageable Georgian restaurants in Moscow: **Guria** (Гурия) on ul. Timura Frunze near Metro: Park Kultury/Парк Културы, and lively **Mama Zoya's** (Мама Зоя) at Sechenovskii/Сеуеновский рer. 8, between Kropotkinskaya and Park Kultury (near Metro:

Kropotkinskaya/Кропоткинская, tel. 201-7743). In both
cases it is advisable to go only for lunch when reservations
are unnecessary. At neither should a full meal cost you more
than $10. Make sure to try *khachapuri* (хачапури—dough
filled with cheese), *pkhali* (пхали—chopped cabbage), and
lobio (Лобио—a bean dish served either hot or cold). Main
dishes are less special—tell them you don't eat meat, order
two or three appetizers per person, and you'll cut down the
size of the bill and still get the best dishes.

Patio Pizza (Патио Пицца)—A large pizza, pasta, and
salad restaurant with red-and-white checked tablecloths and a
huge glassed-in terrace, Patio Pizza seems more a part of
American suburbia than of Moscow. A good all-you-can-eat
salad bar costs $6, whole pizzas start at $5, lasagna or tortellini
is $6 as well, and Visa, MasterCard, and AmEx are accepted
but reservations are not. Come early for dinner to avoid the
lines (daily 12:00–24:00, tel. 201-5000, ul. Volkhonka/
Волхонка 13а, across the street from the Pushkin Museum of
Fine Arts; you can walk from the Kremlin, or take the Metro
to Kropotkinskaya/Кропоткинская, go out the exit towards
the center, and you'll see the Pushkin Museum).

American Bar & Grill (Американский Бар & Гриль)—
Its American, Mexican, and Tex-Mex food attracts both
Russians and foreigners. Salads from $3, burgers from $5,
burritos $7, cheap beverages. Like Patio Pizza, credit cards
but no reservations accepted. The same Venezuelan company
runs both restaurants, as well as Kombi's—Moscow thanks
them (open 24 hours, ul. Tverskaya/Тверская 32, next door
to Kombi's across the street from the Mayakovskaya/
Маяковская Metro exit if you go left at the top of the
escalators).

Rostik's (Ростик'с), on the second floor of GUM in the
northeast corner, is a fast-food chicken restaurant that's very
convenient for sightseers but not worth a special trip. You
pay first and then pick up your meal. It costs only $1.75 to
gnaw on two pieces of roast chicken and a roll, and Cokes
are only 50 cents (daily 10:00–20:00; use the separate
entrance on Sundays).

Café Margarita (Кафе Маргарита)—Named after Mikhail
Bulgakov's novel *The Master and Margarita* and located across
from the corner of Patriarch's Pond where the novel begins,

this is the hangout for Moscow's artsy set, and it's one of the few convenient, attractive, and reasonably inexpensive restaurants that serve Russian food (Malaya Bronnaya/Малая Бронная ul. 28, Metro: Mayakovskaya). Don't be put off if the decorative steel door on the corner is locked; ring the doorbell. Though it's poorly marked and uninviting from the outside, once inside you will feel like you're part of the happening crowd. Lanterns ring the walls, which are covered with original paintings and photographs. The dress and setting are informal—wooden stools and benches. At night you will have to pay a cover charge for the piano player. Tomatoes stuffed with cheese and garlic are the specialty, and for a main course try the *zharkoe po-russki*, which is similar to a beef stew. The menu is in both Russian and English, so ordering should not be a problem (daily 14:00–17:00, 19:00–02:00; sometimes booked for private parties; tel. 299-6534).

Delivery services—Catering mostly to the Western consultant clientele, either **Jack's** (Monday–Friday 10:00–22:00, Saturday and Sunday 11:00–22:00, tel. 281 8263) or **Just Subs** (24 hours, tel. 945-2766) will deliver big submarine sandwiches with your choice of fillings anywhere in town for $6.50 each, $10 minimum order.

Farmer's market—Central Moscow's largest and best market is the Danilovskii Rynok (Даниловский Рынок). Take the Metro one stop south of the Ring on the gray line to Tulskaya/Тульская. Exit toward the center and make your way across the busy intersection to the large circular building with the white, dome-like top.

Supermarkets—These are proliferating in Moscow and it is no longer necessary to trek halfway across the city to find a decent selection of groceries, but here are a few of the best. For reliability, variety, and convenience, the Finnish-run **Stockmann** is still king (daily 10:00–20:00, Zatsepskii/Зацепский Val 4/8; from Metro: Paveletskaya/Павелецкая, facing the Paveletskii railroad station from across the street, walk left for about 3 minutes). The **Arbat Irish House** is closer to the tourist sights, at Novii Arbat/Новыи Арбат 21. It includes a grocery store, a clothing and appliance department, and the Shamrock Bar, and typifies the newer breed of supermarket that caters to Russian shoppers rather than diplomats or other expatriates. From Metro: Arbatskaya/

Арбатская, walk about 3 minutes down Novii Arbat, the street with the monstrous gray Soviet architecture that radiates from the same point as the Arbat pedestrian zone. It's on your left; watch for the green sign. Sneak a look inside the huge Russian grocery store underneath. If you're willing to wait in lines, you can pay less for many of the same products as they have upstairs. Down the street from the Arbat Irish House is the shiny new **Roditi** supermarket (daily 9:00–21:00, tel. 291-2005). Next door to American Express is the **Garden Ring** (daily 9:00–21:00, Bolshaya Sadovaya 1, tel. 209-1572, Metro: Mayakovskaya/Маяковская).

Transportation Connections—Moscow

By Train
Buying tickets in Moscow to points elsewhere is rarely as simple as going up to the ticket window in the respective train station. And rules for foreigners trying to buy train tickets change often and without warning in the capital. Still, price increases mean that tickets are much easier to come by lately. Always remember to bring your passport and visa (although any other piece of photo ID will usually be OK if your passport is at some consulate). Plan on getting a one-way ticket. Round-trip tickets are generally not available, although this could change at any time. Avoid buying tickets from scalpers in train stations. Though their prices are cheap, your name, not theirs, must appear on the ticket.

If you don't want to hassle with buying tickets, the **Travellers Guest House**, whether or not you're staying there, will be happy to get your tickets for you at little or no markup. See Sleeping, above.

By train to destinations within the former Soviet Union, including the Baltics: To get **tickets in advance**, the best place for foreigners to go is the Central Railway Agency at ul. Griboyedova/Грибоедова 6/11. Tickets are sold starting from ten days before the train leaves through the day before the train leaves. From Metro: Turgenevskaya/Тургеневская, walk northeast on ul. Myasnitskaya/Мясницкая, and make your second right onto Griboyedova. Go in building 1, on the right in the fenced-in yard, and visit windows 1 and 2 in the room to the right of the entrance (daily 8:00–13:00, 14:00–19:00). This office is a good place to meet African and Asian students who are studying in Moscow. See how many different languages you can identify.

If it's more convenient, you can also buy advance tickets at the same-day domestic windows of any of the three branches of the Central Railway Agency. One branch is at Leningradskii/ Ленинградский pr. 1, behind Belorusskii Vokzal (station) at Metro: Belorusskaya/Белорусская. You can reach it by crossing the bridge across the tracks to the yellow-and-white building; go in the farthest entrance (marked Кассы). Another branch is at Krasnoprudnaya/Краснопрудная ul. 1, on the first floor of the brown nine-floor apartment building next to Yaroslavskii Vokzal at Metro: Komsomolskaya/Комсомольская. It says Железнодоро-жные Кассы over the door. There's a third office at Mozhaiskii Val 4/6, near Metro: Kievskaya. All three offices are open daily 8:00–13:00 and 14:00–19:00.

For same-day tickets within the former Soviet Union, foreigners must visit one of the three Central Railway Agency branches (see above). Going to **Vilnius**, head to window 1 at the Leningradskii office. To **Riga, Tallinn, or St. Petersburg**, window 2 at the Krasno-prudnaya office is for you.

For same-day or next-day tickets to Tallinn or St. Petersburg only, an excellent option—often the best—is the Intourist windows (19–21, daily approximately 6:00–24:00) on the second floor of Leningradskii Vokzal at Metro: Komsomolskaya/Комсомольская. Go in the main hall of the station, then up the stairs in the far right corner of the hall, through the door on your right, and then to the left.

For the commercial train to St. Petersburg (#36, run by a private firm, not the rail company), tickets are sold at

Station Guide

Trains to:	Leave from:	Nearest Metro:
Warsaw and Vilnius	Belorusskii Vokzal	Belorusskaya/Белорусская
Riga	Rizhskii Vokzal	Rizhskaya/Рижская
Tallinn and St. Petersburg	Leningradskii Vokzal	Komsomolskaya/ Комсомолская

Trains Departing Moscow

#	Destination	Departs	Arrives	2nd class	1st class
158*	St. Petersburg (Санкт-петербург)	12:21	17:20	$25	$46
24	"	12:26	20:25	"	"
48	"	13:25	22:35	"	"
160	"	17:18	23:24	"	"
14	"	20:35	5:10	"	"
28	"	22:00	5:55	"	"
26	"	23:00	7:10	"	"
6	"	23:10	7:35	"	"
2	"	23:55	8:25	"	"
4	"	23:59	8:29	"	"
36	"	0:05	8:50	"	"
20	"	1:00	9:20	"	"
10	"	22:16	6:40	"	"
30	"	1:52	10:33	"	"
176	Tallinn (Таллинн)	16:00	11:05	$38	$73
34	"	17:36	9:55	"	"
1	Riga (Рига)	19:53	11:00	$52	$100
3	"	1:08	12:20	"	"
5	Vilnius (Вильнюс)	17:17	8:30	$45	$87
87	"	19:17	10:40	"	"
32	Helsinki (Хельсинки)	18:17	9:02	$117	$170
9	Warsaw (Варшава)	15:26	8:47	$74	$106

*Friday only, special express.

window 37 in Leningradskii Vokzal, in the same room as the Helsinki windows (see below). This is the only window where you may be able to get return tickets from St. Petersburg (on its sister train, #35), but the staff is sometimes reluctant to sell tickets to foreigners; they told me it was because many theft problems have been reported on this train.

By train to destinations outside the former Soviet Union: For destinations other than Helsinki, you must get tickets at one of the three branches of the Central Railway Agency (see above). Technically, which office you are supposed to go to depends on your destination, but this is not always strictly followed, and one office may sell tickets for another's territory. These offices sell tickets starting 30 days in advance up through the day of departure. For tickets to **Warsaw**, visit window 9 of the office at Leningradskii pr. 1. Tickets to **Mongolia** and **China** are sold at Krasnoprudnaya ul. 1 at windows 5–8. (See the Trans-Siberian Railway chapter for more information.) The third office is at Mozhaiskii Val 4/6.

For Helsinki, tickets are available at windows 35 and 36 in a small special office on the first floor of Leningradskii Vokzal, on the left as you walk into the station's main hall, for $94, $138 first class (daily 8:00–13:00, 14:00–16:00; 16:00–18:30 only for that day's departure). It is cheaper and not much slower to take the train to Tallinn and then the boat to Helsinki. It's also slightly cheaper to go by train to St. Petersburg and then on to Helsinki.

By Air

A taxi to or from Moscow's Sheremetyevo-2 Airport will run you at least $20 and possibly $30. If you can carry your luggage, the alternative is a bus-Metro combination, which takes a long time but costs pennies. Bus #517 runs between Sheremetyevo and Metro: Planernaya/Планерная at the north end of the pink line; bus #551 between Sheremetyevo and Metro: Rechnoi Vokzal/Речной Вокзал at the north end of the green line. You can pay the driver or use Moscow bus tickets (ask them how many you need), but the fare shouldn't be more than $0.50. The bus stop at Sheremetyevo-2 is a short walk out from the terminal, near the parking lot, well past the taxi-Mafia gauntlet. Note that both these bus routes also service the domestic Sheremetyevo-1 terminal on the other side of the runways; don't get off here. If you are coming from the city, it's better to go to Rechnoi Vokzal than to Planernaya.

The following airline numbers may help for reconfirmations and bookings: **British Airways**, Krasnopresnenskaya nab. 12, #1905, tel. 253-2492; **Delta**, Krasnopresnenskaya nab. 12 #1102a, tel. 253-2658 or 253-2659; **Finnair**, Kamergerskii per. 6, tel. 292-8788 or 292-3337; **LOT**, Korovii Val 7, tel. 238-0003 or 238-0313; **Lufthansa**, Olymic Penta Hotel, Olympiiskii Prospekt 18/1, tel. 975-2501; **Malev**, Kamergerskii per. 6, tel. 292-0434 or 229-3515; **SAS**, Kuznetskii Most 3, tel. 925-4747.

ST. PETERSBURG, RUSSIA

Once a swamp, then an imperial capital, and now a showpiece of vanished aristo-cratic opulence shot through with the grimy ruins of socialism, St. Petersburg is Russia's most accessible and most tourist-worthy city. Standing in Palace Square, you'll shiver and think, "The revolution start-ed *here*." (You may also shiver and think, "I'm as far north as Alaska.") Palaces, gardens, statues, and arched bridges over graceful canals bring back the time of the czars. One of the world's greatest art museums tops it off. Amid such artistic and historical splendor, modern Russia and its problems seem terribly out of place, but here they are: streets of legless beggars, Mafia-controlled kiosks, wheezing buses, shabby bread stores, broken signs, exhaust-stained facades, pornog-raphy dealers, and ice-cream stands in see-your-breath weather.

Compared to Moscow, St. Petersburg is compact, walkable, friendly, manageable, and architecturally intact. Don't get overly uptight about timing your visit to the summer solstice for St. Petersburg's much-bandied "White Nights." You'll be able to enjoy bright evenings here all summer long. If you want the real midnight sun, go to Finland.

Save a sunny day just to walk. Keep your head up: ugly Soviet shops mar the first floor of nearly every build-ing, but the upper facades are sun-warmed and untouched by street grime. Make sure you get off Nevsky Prospekt to explore the back streets along the canals. Visit the Summer Gardens. Climb St. Isaac's Cathedral for the view. The next day, when the Baltic Sea brings clouds and drizzle, plunge into the Hermitage or the Russian Museum.

Planning Your Time

Day 1

10:00 After breakfast, take a leisurely walk down Nevsky Prospekt to acquaint yourself with the city.

11:00 Climb up St. Isaac's Cathedral and peek inside too.
12:00 Walk back to Sadko's for lunch.
13:30 The Russian Museum is just up the street.
18:30 Retire to the Korean House for dinner.

Day 2
10:30 Plunge into the Hermitage.
13:30 Take the Metro to the Schwabskii Domik for their
      lunch special.
15:00 Take the Metro to the Peter and Paul Fortress.

Day 3 (optional)
Spend more time in the Hermitage, visit the Piskaryovskoe
cemetery, or go to Petrodvorets for the day.

St. Petersburg

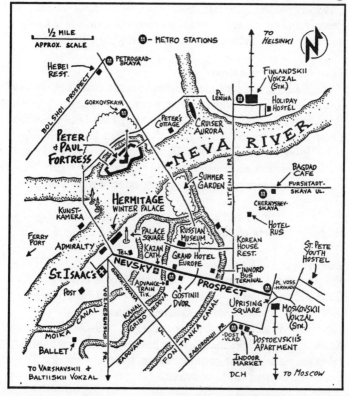

Orientation
(tel. code: 7812; tel. code within Baltics and Russia: 8812)

Get to know **Nevsky Prospekt** (Невский Проспект), St. Petersburg's main street. Almost everything you'll want to see is either along Nevsky or between it and the river. A few spots, like the Finland train station and the Peter and Paul Fortress, are just across the river.

Nevsky starts at the slender-spired Admiralty, next to the river and the Winter Palace. Running outward from the city it crosses three canals: first the Moika (Мойка), then Kanal Griboyedova (Канал Грибоедова), and finally the Fontanka (Фонтанка). Tourist Nevsky ends a little farther out at Ploshchad Vosstaniya (Uprising Square, Площадь Восстания), home to a tall obelisk and the Moskovskii train station.

Walking distances are manageable (from Ploshchad Vosstaniya to the Admiralty takes only 30–45 minutes), and St. Petersburg has enough natural landmarks that on a nice summer day you can get around on foot even without a map.

Tourist Information

Peter T.i.P.S., run by a travel agency, is the closest thing to a tourist information office that St. Pete's has to offer (Monday–Friday 10:00–20:00, Saturday 10:00–18:00, Nevsky Prospekt 86, located across from the Nevsky Palace Hotel, tel. 279-0037, fax 275-0806). They give out tourist info and book theater tickets, cruises, bus tours, and hotel rooms. For $20 their visa service will send you a letter of invitation for a single-entry visa.

For a helpful and entertaining locally produced English-language guidebook, buy the *Fresh Guide to St. Petersburg.*

Currency Exchange

Everywhere. The **American Express** office is inside the Grand Hotel Europe (Monday–Friday 9:00–17:00, Saturday 9:00–13:00, Mikhailovskaya/Михайловская ul. 1, Metro: Nevsky Prospekt/Невский Проспект, tel. 119-6009). Surprisingly, their exchange desk has reasonable rates and takes only a 1 percent commission on traveler's checks. They do all the normal AmEx services.

Mail and Telephones

The central post office is at Pochtamtskaya/Почтамтская ul. 9, under the arch a couple of blocks down from St. Isaac's Cathedral. Send international mail from window 25 (Monday–Saturday 9:00–20:00, Sunday 10:00–18:00).

Public phones use the same tokens as the Metro. Brand-new, bright green "Great Nordic" telephones have recently sprouted along the streets of St. Petersburg. These phones, good for local or long-distance calls, take a phone card (available at T.i.P.S. and offices throughout the city— the most central at Nevsky Prospekt 27, tel. 274-9383). Cards cost a minimum of $6.50 and have an expiration date. Using a phone card, calls to the States run $3.50/minute; to Europe, $1.50/minute.

You can also make long-distance calls at the central telephone office at ul. Gertsena/Герцена 5, between Palace Square and Nevsky Prospekt on the street with the big arches. (This street is due to be renamed Bolshaya Morskaya ul., but hasn't been yet.) The entrance is between the two blue mailboxes. For calls within the ex-U.S.S.R., go to the right as you enter; a booth sells wide-grooved tokens for the intercity phones in the surrounding booths. In 1995, one 25-cent token bought 2 minutes to Moscow or the Baltics. (Open 24 hours.) For international calls, go through the wooden gates on the left. Pick up a cork-like numbered token, go to the cabin with that number, make your call, push the "Ответ" button when the other side answers, and pay afterwards. Calls to America cost about $2.50/minute; to Europe, $1.50/minute. (Daily 8:00–23:00.)

American Consulate

Furshtadtskaya/Фурштадтская ul. 15, Metro: Chernyshevskaya/Чернышевская, tel. 275-1701. American citizen services Monday–Friday 9:00–17:30.

Bookstore

The Soviet-era international bookshop at Nevsky Prospekt 13, near Palace Square, has lots of new and used art books and trashy English fiction, as well as St. Petersburg maps at better prices than the outdoor stalls (Monday–Friday 10:00–14:00 and 15:00–19:00).

St. Petersburg Metro

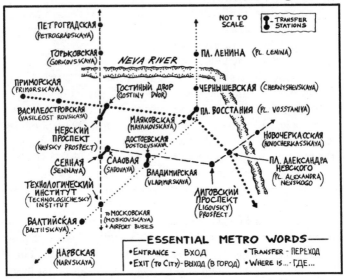

ПЕТРОГРАДСКАЯ (PETROGRADSKAYA)

ГОРЬКОВСКАЯ (GORKOVSKAYA) — *NEVA RIVER*

ПРИМОРСКАЯ (PRIMORSKAYA)

ПЛ. ЛЕНИНА (PL. LENINA)

ЧЕРНЫШЕВСКАЯ (CHERNYSHEVSKAYA)

ГОСТИННЫЙ ДВОР (GOSTINY DVOR)

ВАСИЛЕОСТРОВСКАЯ (VASILEOST ROVSKAYA)

ПЛ. ВОССТАНИЯ (PL. VOSSTANIYA)

МАЯКОВСКАЯ (MAYAKOVSKAYA)

НЕВСКИЙ ПРОСПЕКТ (NEVSKY PROSPECT)

ДОСТОЕВСКАЯ (DOSTOEVSKAYA)

НОВОЧЕРКАССКАЯ (NOVOCHERKASSKAYA)

СЕННАЯ (SENNAYA) — САДОВАЯ (SADOVAYA)

ВЛАДИМИРСКАЯ (VLADIMIRSKAYA)

ПЛ. АЛЕКСАНДРА НЕВСКОГО (PL. ALEXANDRA NEVSKOGO)

ТЕХНОЛОГИЧЕСКИЙ ИНСТИТУТ (TECHNOLOGICHESKY INSTITUT)

ЛИГОВСКИЙ ПРОСПЕКТ (LIGOVSKY PROSPECT)

to МОСКОВСКАЯ (MOSKOVSKAYA) + AIRPORT BUSES

БАЛТИЙСКАЯ (BALTIISKAYA)

НАРВСКАЯ (NARVSKAYA)

NOT TO SCALE — TRANSFER STATIONS

—ESSENTIAL METRO WORDS—
- Entrance – ВХОД
- Exit (to City) – ВЫХОД (В ГОРОД)
- Transfer – ПЕРЕХОД
- Where is… – ГДЕ…

Getting Around St. Petersburg

The Metro is not that helpful for getting around the center of the city, but essential for longer trips. It requires metal tokens which you can buy at station entrances, and which also work in the pay phones. Trams and buses can be quite useful, but it takes some time to familiarize yourself with stops and routes. The best way to do so is to buy the partially bilingual Municipal Transport Routes map published by the city's Culture and Tourism Committee. Other maps have more English and street detail but don't list transport lines. Good map sources are the big Dom Knigi bookstore at Nevsky Prospekt 28 (maps are on the second floor), the smaller bookstore at Nevsky 13, or street stalls, although these often charge higher prices.

Sights—St. Petersburg

▲▲▲The Hermitage (Эрмитаж)—Ranking up there with the Louvre in Paris and the Prado in Madrid, the Hermitage's vast collection of European masters makes it one of the world's top art museums (foreigners are charged $9, students $6). Modern art is on the top floor, antiquities at ground level, and everything in between on the second floor. Don't miss the exciting cache of recently unveiled paintings Russia appropriated from Germany near the end of WWII. This Impressionist and Post-Impressionist art features such "light"-weights as Renoir and Monet.

The attraction of the Hermitage is not only the art, but also the begilded, bedraped, and bejeweled rooms themselves. The museum is in the czars' old Winter Palace, the green-and-white building between Palace Square and the river. In 1917, the Provisional Government met for the very last time in the green-pillared Malachite Hall, before being arrested in the adjacent dining room. The building faces Palace Square, where Bolshevik forces assembled before storming in. The museum entrance is on the other, river-front side of the building (Tuesday–Sunday 10:30–18:00; ticket windows close an hour before the museum; the top floor closes 40 minutes early).

The number of people employed at the Hermitage is also amazing—practically each one of the hundreds of rooms has an attendant, and there are at least a dozen people working in the coat-check department. Local guides are cheap, eager, and helpful. Try Alexandra Ivanova (who gives Hermitage tours, gets cheap tickets for concerts and ballets, and even takes people to the airport $10/hr, tel. 232-6458), Victor (586-2348), and Alexy Alyoshetkin (who tailors sightseeing to your needs, tel. 543-8475).

▲▲**Russian Museum** (Русский Музей)—Here's a fascinating collection of prerevolutionary Russian art, particularly 18th- and 19th-century painting and portraiture. People who complain that the Hermitage is just more Monets and Rembrandts love the Russian Museum, since the artists are less well-known in the West. Much of the work reveals Russians exploring their own landscape: marshes, birch stands, muddy village streets, the conquest of Siberia, firelit scenes in family huts, and Repin's portrait of Tolstoy standing barefoot in the woods. You may enjoy Rerikh, an early 20th-century Russian artist who painted startling, imaginary, Himalayan landscapes in icy blue colors. Entrance to the museum is currently through an unmarked door to the right of the main staircase ($6.50, free the first Wednesday of every month; Wednesday–Sunday 10:00–18:00, Monday 10:00-17:00; ticket window

closes an hour before the museum; Inzhenernaya/
Инженерная ul. 4, a block off Nevsky behind the Grand
Hotel Europe).

▲▲**St. Isaac's Cathedral** (Исаакиевский Собор)—Head
down ul. Gogolya (i.e., Malaya Morskaya) from Nevsky
Prospekt. There are separate entrances for the cathedral and
for the colonnade stairway that leads to the roof. Russians buy
tickets at the booth outside the fence (cathedral $0.20, colon-
nade $0.10); foreigners have to go inside the cathedral and buy
tickets at a special desk. At $9 for the church, $4.50 for the
colonnade (students half price), I'd simply take a peek at the
massive 19th-century interior while you buy your cheaper
colonnade ticket. The view from the rooftop is worth the climb
and the money. (Thursday–Monday 11:00–19:00, colonnade
stairway closes at 17:00; Tuesday 11:00–18:00, colonnade closes at 16:00.) St. Isaac's is a museum, not a functioning house of
worship; if you want to see an Orthodox service, take the
Metro to pl. Aleksandra Nevskovo (Пл. Александра Невского)
and visit the church in the *lavra* (seminary) across the street
from the Metro exit—there's a service daily at 18:00, and it
doesn't cost anything. There's a $0.75 entrance fee for the
cemetery, where you can see Dostoevsky's grave.

▲▲**Nevsky Prospekt itself**—Nevsky's architectural high-
lights include the magnificent arch of the General Staff
Building down Bolshaya Morskaya ul., the Kazan Cathedral,
and the views down the canals. You should also check out
the sign at Nevsky 14, preserved from World War II, warning citizens that the north side of the street was more dan-
gerous during shelling. Nevsky is better known as Russia's
premier shopping street. The building with the distinctive
tower at #28 is the city's main Dom Knigi (bookstore).
There's a Melodiya (Мелодия) store at #34 which stocks the
same few classical CDs that are sold everywhere else in the
country; if you still use your record player, pick up some
dirt-cheap East German classical LPs here or the latest
Russian pop releases. Farther on you can find stores selling
crystal and artwork, and there's an opulent fur shop at #57
in the Nevsky Palace Hotel. At #65 is a representative hard-
ware store, while Reebok has opened an outlet at #75, ironi-
cally next door to a food store (#73) which uses the old
three-line system.

▲**Peter and Paul Fortress** (Петропавловская Крепость)—Founded by Peter the Great in 1703 during the Great Northern War with Sweden, this fortress on an island in the Neva was the birthplace of the city of St. Petersburg. With its gold steeple catching the sunlight and its blank walls facing the Winter Palace across the river, the place is almost nicer to look at than to visit. You can wander through and climb the bastions for free. Your ticket lets you into the church (where Peter is buried), the jail (which housed numerous 19th-century revolutionaries including Lenin's older brother), and several museum-style exhibits. The main entrance is through the park from Metro: Gorkovskaya/Горьковская. Buy tickets inside the museum gift shop opposite the church ($3, students half-price, Thursday–Tuesday 11:00–17:00, closed the last Tuesday of each month; ticket window closes an hour before the fortress).

Moored in the river along Petrogradskaya nab. not far from the fortress is the Cruiser *Aurora* (Крейсер "Аврора"), which fired the shot that signalled the start of the Russian Revolution. Now a museum, it's worth visiting if you are a history buff or Bolshevik (free, Tuesday–Thursday and Saturday–Sunday 10:30–16:00, no English descriptions).

Halfway between the fortress and the *Aurora*, at Petrovskaya nab. 6, is Peter the Great's log cabin, entombed in a small 19th-century brick house in a tiny park. Peter lived here briefly in 1703; inside you can see modest exhibits on his life and the building of St. Petersburg ($1.25, Russians $0.12, Wednesday–Monday 10:00–18:00, closed the last Monday of each month).

▲**Dostoevski Museum** (Музей ф. М. Достоевского)— Although much of the furnishings are gone, you can get some feel for how the famous writer lived from visiting the six-room apartment where he wrote *The Brothers Karamazov*. Captions are in English. The *babushki* who run the place put a new half-cup of tea on Dostoevski's desk every morning ($2.50, CIS citizens $0.04, Tuesday–Sunday 11:00–18:30, last entry 17:30, closed the last Wednesday of every month; Kuznechii/Кузнечый рer. 5, a block from Metro: Dostoevskaya/Достоевская). The Museum of the Arctic is across the street.

▲**Piskaryovskoe Memorial Cemetery** (Пискарёвское Мемориальное Кладбище)—This is a memorial to the hundreds of thousands who died in the city during the German siege of Leningrad in World War II. The cemetery, with its eternal flame, acres of mass grave bunkers (marked only with the year of death), moving statue of Mother Russia, and many pilgrims bringing flowers to remember lost loved ones, is an awe-inspiring experience even for an American tourist to whom the siege of Leningrad is just another page from the history books. To get there, take the Metro north to Ploshchad Muzhestva (Площадь Мужества), exit, walk through the large brick apartment complex to the street, cross it to the eastbound bus stop, and take bus #123 to the sixth stop—you'll see the buildings on your left.

▲**Kunstkamera** (Кунсткамера)—This is officially known as the Peter the Great Museum of Anthropology and Ethnography. Truthfully, though, most people come only for the collection of hideously deformed preserved fetuses that Peter the Great bought from an Amsterdam doctor and had brought back to Russia. The rest is a vast, dusty, poorly lit collection of Soviet-era dioramas and displays on world cultures. Check out the excellent American Indian section, the "Our Baltic Neighbors" display, or the selection of photographs of socialist Africa's public buildings. No English captions. ($2, Russians $0.30, Sunday–Thursday 11:00–18:00, Universitetskaya nab. 3, in the blue-and-white building across the big bridge from the Hermitage.)

▲▲**A musical evening**—Keep an eye out for ballet and opera performances. The Marinskii (formerly Kirov) Ballet performs in Teatralnaya Ploshchad (Театральная Площадь). The Malii Opera is on Italyanskaya/Итальянская by the Russian Museum. If you don't want to brave the box office, your hostel or hotel may be able to help you with tickets. Otherwise, go to the theater 30–45 minutes before the show and stand in line with everyone else for cheap balcony seats. If that fails, scalpers sell tickets for about $10. Summertime means tours and infrequent performances.

▲▲**Peterhof** (Петергоф)—If you have time for a day trip, consider Peter the Great's lavish palace at Peterhof, also known as Petrodvorets (Петродворец), along the Gulf of Finland west of the city. This is Russia's Versailles and the target of many tour groups and travel poster photographers. In summer, hydrofoils leave for the palace every half-hour during the daytime from a dock near the Hermitage. In winter, you have to take a suburban train and then switch to a bus—ask for details (11:00–8:00, closed Monday and last Tuesday of month).

Sleeping in St. Petersburg
(tel. code: 7812; tel. code within Baltics and Russia: 8812)

Hostels
St. Petersburg International Hostel is a normal hostel like those in Western Europe, with friendly English-speaking staff, 60 beds in clean three- to five-bed rooms with clean showers, a members' kitchen, a small shop, a cybercafé for Internet addicts, Western movies every night, and a fairly strict set of rules (shoes off in the bathroom, small fine for coming in after the midnight curfew, etc.). Fifteen dollars a night includes continental breakfast. The hostel will reserve train tickets for you; they get the best deal they can find and then add a $5 reservation fee. They're busy in summer, so reserve ahead by phone (tel. 329-8018, fax 329-8019, e-mail ryh@ryh.spb.su.) or through the hostel's overseas agents, listed below. The hostel itself is now an accredited agent of the International Youth Hostel Federation.

The hostel, at 3rd Sovetskaya/3я Советская ul. 28, is about a 10-minute walk from Nevsky Prospekt, Ploshchad Vosstaniya, the Moskovskii Vokzal (train station), and the associated Metro stations. Coming out the front door of the train station, walk right, heading into the major street (with overhead trolley wires) that runs between the two electronic billboards. Take your first left off this street onto Suvorovskii/Суворовский pr. Walk two blocks (past the blue signs of the Philips housewares store) and then turn right onto 3rd Sovetskaya ul. (which is supposed to be renamed 3rd Rozhdestvenskaya/3я Рождественская ul. at some point). The hostel is the remodeled cream-and-magenta building half a block down on your left.

Downstairs you'll see Sindbad Travel, a budget and student travel agency linked to Council Travel in the U.S. Run

by the hostel, Sindbad sells train and air tickets, and offers a
25 percent discount on tickets to Helsinki (tel. 327-8384 or
329-8019, e-mail sindbad@ryh.spb.su.).

The best thing about the St. Petersburg International
Hostel is its efficient system of visa support. If you're in
the U.S.A. or Canada, the St. Petersburg Hostel office in
Redondo Beach, California, will take your reservations and
get your visa for you. Outside the U.S.A. or Canada, contact
the hostel or the California office directly by fax, or go in
person to one of its agents in Finland, Germany, England,
Estonia, and Lithuania. You will receive a reservation form
which you (or the agent) will fax to the hostel; when the hostel
returns your confirmed and stamped reservation form, you
can take or send it to the nearest Russian consulate or embassy
to get your visa. You will usually receive visa support for ten
days longer than you plan to stay in the hostel, which gives
you the flexibility to stay longer without ridiculous extension hassles.

They will also take reservations for Holiday Hostel in
St. Petersburg, Travellers Guest House in Moscow, and any
future hostels that may open in Russia (there are plans for
one in Irkutsk) and give visa support for your time there. In
the summertime they are busy; if there's no room left they
will confirm you for Holiday Hostel.

The hostel can also provide business and multiple-entry
visas, which are more flexible than tourist visas. Tourist visas
can be extended one time only in St. Petersburg, for no
more than three days, but business visas can be extended up
to three months, and multiple-entry visas, though expensive,
are valid up to one year.

The hostel's mailing address is P.O. Box 8, SF53501
Lappeenranta, Finland, but it's faster to contact them by fax,
phone, or e-mail (see above). Their World Wide Web address,
which includes an online edition of the *St. Petersburg Press* and
the *Fresh Guide to St. Petersburg*, is http://www.spb.su/ryh.

The hostel's handy American office is at 409 N. Pacific
Coast Highway, Bldg. #106, Suite 390, Redondo Beach, CA
90277 (tel. 310/618-2014, fax 310/618-1140, 71573.2010
@compuserve.com). You can also contact their agents in
Finland at Eurohostel (Linnankatu 9, Helsinki, tel. 664
452); in Germany at DJH (Tempelhofer Ufer 32, Berlin,

tel. 264-9520); in England at the YHA Travel Store (14 Southampton St., London, tel. 836-1036); in Estonia at Karol Travel Agency (Lembitu tn. 4, Tallinn, tel. 313 918); or in Lithuania at the Lithuanian YHA (Kauno 1a-407, Vilnius, tel. 262 660). For example, if you make your booking at Helsinki's Eurohostel on Monday, the hostel will fax back your confirmed reservation form that same evening, you can go to the Russian consulate on Tuesday, and you will have your visa on Thursday at the latest (or the same day if you pay extra). Eurohostel charges a flat fee of 150mk for the booking, which includes all necessary faxes and your first night in St. Petersburg.

If in the U.S.A. or Canada, call, write, or fax the California office and they will mail you a reservation form and information package. To get your Russian visa, they charge a $10 reservation fee, a $30 visa service fee, and as little as $30 for your visa (more if you need it quickly). You'll also pay $15 for each night you plan to stay at the hostel. You should plan to work at least four weeks in advance; faster processing is possible but more expensive.

If you are contacting the hostel by fax or e-mail, it will save time if your first communication includes your full legal name; citizenship; birthdate; passport number and expiration date; dates you plan to stay at the hostel; place, date, and means of entry into Russia; place, date, and means of exit from Russia; Visa or MasterCard number; your name as it is written on the credit card; card expiration date; and signature. They will then use this information to fill out the reservation form, which they'll fax to you and which you can then take to the Russian consulate yourself to get your tourist visa. The hostel will charge you $31, which includes your first night at the hostel.

Holiday Hostel has more doubles, is cheaper in the off-season, has more congenial common space, is less strict (no curfew), and has a nicer view than the International Hostel. On the other hand, the bathrooms are not as modern, the door is harder to find and get into, the hostel is not as tightly run, and it is beyond walking distance from Nevsky Prospekt (ul. Mikhailova/Михайлова 1, tel./fax 542 7364, mailing address: P.O. Box 19, St. Petersburg 195009, Russia). Holiday Hostel has about a hundred beds in two-to five-bed rooms on several floors of a larger building, and charges $12–$14 per person per night, depending on the season. Breakfast is included and laundry service is available.

The hostel is less than a 5-minute walk from the Ploshchad Lenina (Площадь Ленина) Metro station at the Finlyandskii Vokzal (train station). Coming out the front door of the Metro station, walk straight down through the park to the river, then turn left one block to ul. Mikhailova; the hostel is in the building on the far left corner with the fourth-floor corner balcony. The hostel entrance is in the inside corner of the L-shaped building; go in through the archway off of ul. Mikhailova, look for the "YH" sign on the wall, and ring the bell—the hostel is on the third floor. The entrance code is 1648. Holiday Hostel says they can also provide visa support by fax, independent of the International Hostel.

One foreign students' dormitory, which has space for 270 people, is a great deal—but ask if the hot water's working. The dorm, part of the Leningrad Pedagogical University, formerly housed foreigners who were being trained as teachers of Russian; now it rents out many of its rooms to travelers. Singles cost about $19, doubles start at $19, and two-room quads run $32 (all with private bath). It's located steps off Nevsky Prospekt past the Kazan Cathedral, about two blocks from Metro: Nevsky Prospekt/Невский Проспект, at ul. Plekhanova/Плеханова 6 (tel. 314-7472). Go in the door by the nameplate marked "Факултет." The dorm cannot provide any help with visa support, but is a fair option for people who are already in Russia.

Hotels

The St. Petersburg hotel scene is frustrating. The cheaper hotels—with doubles under $50—are usually too sleazy or too far from the Metro. Hotels with new furniture, appealing bathrooms, and a modern lobby start at $100 for a double, and even that often means a pompous Soviet-style reception desk, congealed breakfast, distant location, and shady characters in the lobby who possibly drive the $40,000 cars without license plates that are parked outside. What's more, these hotels generally aren't together enough to fax you an invitation letter to support your visa application. For enlightened service, propriety, and visa support in the center of the city, there are first-world fortresses such as the Nevsky Palace (tel. 311-6366), the Grand Hotel Europe (119-6000), and the Astoria (311-4206), but they cost upwards of $200 a night. Though its rooms are small, a better deal is the Swiss-run **Hotelship Peterhof** at nab. Makarova 24 (tel. 213-6321, fax 950-1406) which costs $100 per person per night (reserve at 415/398-7947 in the U.S.A., 41/55/272 755, fax 272 788 in Switzerland). In the cheaper price category the following hotel is the only one I can recommend:

  Hotel Rus (Гостиница Русь) is encouraging: a large, clean, inexpensive, half-modern hotel on a quiet street just blocks from Nevsky Prospekt, and there are no goons in the lobby (Artilleriiskaya/Артиллерийская ul. 1, Metro: Chernyshevskaya/Чернышевская, tel. 273-4683). Built for the 1980 Olympics, it's definitely one of the world's ugliest hotels, but the rooms are standard and the lobby is surprisingly welcoming. Doubles with bath cost $40, but the "luxury" two-room doubles are definitely worth the extra money at only $50. The bathrooms are typically Soviet, but OK. Breakfast $3.

Private Rooms

Petropolitana Tours, at Zaslanova 4 (From Metro: Ligovskii Prospekt follow the wall to the tracks, go across the tracks, and follow blue-and-white signs with yellow arrow, tel. 812/311-0988, fax 164-8909), charges from $10–$15 for a room with a family, from $20 for a whole apartment. For rooms with a host family, they give you the address and you pay a representative who meets you there. Pickup at the train station costs extra. Visa support possible.

  The **Travellers Guest House in Moscow** can find you a home-stay in St. Petersburg that will meet your train and that charges $10 a night without breakfast (tel. in Moscow 971-4059, fax 280-7686, e-mail tgh@glas.apc.org).

  Host Families Association is run by a St. Petersburg Technical Institute professor (tel./fax 275-1992) and overpriced at $25–$30 per person per night. They meet you at the train or the airport and only then tell you your host family's address. Claims to be able to provide visa support documentation.

Eating in St. Petersburg

The listings below are your best bets for good food served
honestly for $5–$10 a meal. Since St. Petersburg water is so
bad, and since your time here may be limited, I suggest you
spend extra money on safe, reliable restaurants that use filtered water rather than extra time looking for bargains.

Recommended Eateries

Koreiskii Domik (Корейский Домик, i.e., Korean House)—
A full meal runs about $6–$7 per person, including tea, rice,
spicy pickled vegetables, and an entree like *chapche* (noodles
with vegetables and meat), *lapsha* (noodles and meat in
broth), or *pulgogi* (spicy Korean-style meat cooked on a
burner on your table). Quick service, English menu. And I've
drunk their filtered water and never gotten sick. In summer
especially, try to reserve at tel. 259-9333 (daily 13:00–21:00,
Izmailovskii Prospekt/Иэмайловский Проспект 2, near
Metro: Tekhnologicheskii Institut/Технологиуеский
Институт.

Sadko's, the cheapest of the three restaurants in the
Grand Hotel Europe, is St. Petersburg's yuppie American
hangout. Inside it feels like Manhattan. The menu is chalked
on blackboards, and parts of it vary daily. Appetizers, which
are sometimes a light meal in themselves, cost about $5,
main dishes cost $8–$10, and desserts cost $4. Tax and serv-
ice are included, so this is what you actually pay. Beverages
are expensive (Cokes, $3). AmEx, Visa, and MasterCard
accepted. No non-smoking section. Reserve for dinner on
weekends, when there's live music and a big crowd. Ask a
lady at the bar what her name is, and she'll answer "$200."
(Daily 12:00–1:00, last orders at 00:30; at the corner of
Nevsky Prospekt and ul. Mikhailovskaya/Михайловская,
almost across the street from Gostinii Dvor; tel. 119-6000
ext. 6390 for reservations.)

Le Café, formerly a state-run bakery, has been renovated
and transformed into three modern shops with separate
entrances (Nevsky Prospekt 142, at the corner of Degtyarnaya/
Дегтярная ul; recommended for those staying at the St.
Petersburg International Hostel, which is 3 blocks away).
The stand-up café serves edible though not very good pizza
for $1.50 and Middle Eastern *shawarma* sandwiches for $1.25

(daily 11:00–21:00). The bar and restaurant are pricey, but you can get a hamburger with fries for $6 (daily 12:00–24:00). The new private Петрохлеб bakery has a good selection of bread, rolls, and pastries on serve-yourself shelves (Monday-Saturday 9:00–14:00 and 15:00–20:00, Sunday 9:00–14:00 and 15:00–19:00; Metro: Ploshchad Vosstaniya/ Площадь Восстания, then walk about 2 blocks away from the center of town).

Palatable

Bagdad (Багдад)—Order at the counter. The thing to get is *lagman* (a filling soup with meat, vegetables, beans, and noodles for under $2) plus a round *kul'cha* roll. If you're hungry, add on an order of *plov* (meat pilaf, $1.50) or *manty* (dumplings, $2). There are only four tables, though, and no bathrooms, so it's best for a quick, informal lunch or dinner (daily 11:00–23:00, Furshtadtskaya/Фурштадтская ul. 35, downstairs from the street, Metro: Chernyshevskaya/ Чернышевская).

    Nevsky 40 (Невский 40)—There are nicer places to eat in town than this German-style bar and restaurant, but it's convenient and you can get a plate of spaghetti for $4 (daily 12:00–24:00, Nevsky Prospekt 40).

    Schwabski Domik (Швабский Домик)—More German food. Come for the $6.40 lunch special served from 11:00–17:00; for example, soup, sausages with sauerkraut and potatoes, and a bottle of German beer. It's large, so there's usually no need to reserve. Armed security guard by the coat check. AmEx, Visa, and MasterCard accepted. Also has a cheaper but less appetizing stand-up buffet. (Daily 11:00–2:00, Novocherkasskaya pl. 19. Right at Metro: Novocherkasskaya/Новочеркасская; go up stairway #8; tel. 528-2211.)

    Tbilisi (Тбилиси) serves Georgian food. The decor and atmosphere are not particularly attractive but the food is edible, the service acceptable, and you can get a full meal for less than $10. There's an English menu: a typical meal might include *kharcho* soup, *lobio* (beans) or a meat entree, and *lavash* bread. It's very close to the Peter and Paul Fortress and Metro: Gorkovskaya/Горьковская, but bring a map. Reserve for dinner at 232 9391 (daily 12:00–22:00, Sytninskaya/Сытнинская ul. 10).

Expatriates enjoy Chinese food at **Shenyan** (ul.
Rubenshteina/Рубинштейна 12, just off Nevsky Prospekt,
tel. 113-2356) and the restaurant at **Nevsky Prospekt 86**,
which runs an excellent beer garden in the summer.

Picnics

Farmer's market—A trip here will show you the true scope
of Russia's agricultural richness (and fill your picnic basket).
St. Petersburg's best and most central farmer's market is at
Kuznechii/Кузнечый per., right across the street from the
Dostoevski museum (look for the big Рынок sign; Metro:
Vladimirskaya/Владимирская). Any Russian farmer's market
is worth a visit even if you're not shopping. First you'll pass
babushki selling plastic bags, then Georgians shouting
"Molodoi chelovyek!" (young man) and *"Devushka!"* (young
lady) as they try to entice you towards their piles of oranges,
tomatoes, cucumbers, and pears. In the honey (Мёд) section,
a chorus line of white-aproned *babushki* stands ready to let
you dip and test each kind. Check out the barrels of sauer-
kraut and trays of pickled garlic and cabbage. In the herbs
section, you can sniff massive bunches of fresh coriander
(кинза) and wade through a lifetime of horseradish (хрен);
nearby, look for a Central Asian spice trader with wares of
every color laid out in little bags.

    Supermarkets—St. Petersburg has an improving array
of supermarkets and grocery stores with goods on open
shelves; discouragingly, they tend to carry only imported
products. Two of the biggest and best are run by Finnish
chains. **Stockmann** has a store at Finlyandskii/ Финляндский pr. 1 (daily 10:00–21:00), across the street from the
round building of the Hotel St. Petersburg and across the
Sampsonievskii Most (bridge) from the Cruiser *Aurora*. This
is about three stops on tram #6 from either Metro: Gorkovs-
kaya/Горьковская or Ploshchad Lenina/Площадь Ленина, or
you can walk. More convenient to the Metro but with a
slightly poorer selection and less English labeling is **Spar**
(daily 10:00–21:00) at Metro: Narvskaya/Нарвская, in the
first floor of a five-story pinkish-orange building across the
street from the Metro exit.

    On and around Nevsky Prospekt there are several
smaller corner groceries with open shelves. Try the one in

the basement of Nevsky 48 (daily to 22:00) or at Nevsky 76 (daily until midnight, on the corner of Liteinii Prospekt).

Transportation Connections— St. Petersburg

By Train
To Moscow, trains leave from the Moskovskii Vokzal (Московский Вокзал, Moscow Station), Metro: Ploshchad Vosstaniya/Площадь восстания.

To the Baltics, trains leave from the Varshavskii Vokzal (Варшавский Вокзал, Warsaw Station). Metro: Baltiiskaya/Балтийская actually brings you to a different station, the confusingly named Baltiiskii Vokzal; from the Metro exit, walk to the main street, turn right, and walk one long block to the Varshavskii Vokzal.

To Helsinki, trains leave from Finlyandskii Vokzal (Финляндский Вокзал, Finland Station, Metro: Ploshchad Lenina/Площадь Ленина).

Buying Tickets
Tickets for all trains are available without too much hassle at the Central Railway Booking Office (Monday–Saturday 8:00–20:00, Sunday 8:00–16:00, Kanal Griboyedova/Канал Грибоедова 24). This is across the canal from the Kazan Cathedral and just a few doors from Nevsky Prospekt. Look for the steam engine sign above the building. Metro: Nevsky Prospekt/Невский Проспект.

Only Russian citizens are officially allowed to buy tickets from the windows in the main ground-floor hall. Foreigners should go to the right and up the stairs next to the women's bathroom (follow the Intourist signs) to the second floor. The clerks do not speak English. They need to write your last name on the ticket in Cyrillic, and the easiest way to help them do this is to bring your passport and visa, but if you can't do that, any other ID (such as an American driver's license) is usually OK. Windows 103 and 104 sell advance and same-day tickets for destinations within the former Soviet Union, including the Baltic states (you have to pay at window 92 or 97, then return to pick up your ticket). An exception is the "commercial train" (#35/36) to Moscow, for which you have

Trains Departing St. Petersburg

#	Destination	Departs	Arrives	2nd class	1st class
47	Moscow (Москва)	8:35	18:45	$33	$63
157*	"	12:15	17:17	"	"
23	"	13:05	22:09	"	"
159	"	15:50	21:51	"	"
19	"	20:20	5:16	"	"
27	"	22:30	6:45	"	"
9	"	22:45	7:10	"	"
25	"	23:10	7:15	"	"
5	"	23:33	7:43	"	"
35	"	23:38	8:52	"	"
1	"	23:55	8:25	"	"
3	"	23:59	8:30	"	"
13	"	0:35	10:07	"	"
17	Tallinn (Таллинь)	21:41	5:50	$22	$39
649	"	23:33	8:44	"	"
37	Riga (Рига)	22:00	9:20	$42	$80
191	Vilnius (Вильнюс)	22:25	11:59	$34	$63
33**	Helsinki (Хельсинки)	8:05	15:03	$65	$98
35***	"	15:55	21:26	"	"

*Thursday only, special ER-200 fast train.

**Russian-run *Repin*.

***Finn-run *Sibelius*.

to visit window 100. Round-trip tickets (e.g., to Moscow) are impossible to get. Students at Russian universities can visit windows 101 and 102 for lower rates. Window 94 sells tickets to Finland; window 99 sells tickets to Germany, while tickets to Poland are handled by windows 80 and 81 back down on the ground floor. To get your money back on tickets you don't want, visit window 86. (These window numbers may change.)

For a $5 markup over ticket price, the St. Petersburg International Hostel will buy train tickets for any traveler (though hostel guests reportedly receive better service).

Same-day tickets (except to Finland) are available at the Central Railway Booking Office (windows 103 and 104). You can also buy same-day tickets at the departing train station (within 24 hours of departure), but these are a headache. For same-day tickets at Moskovskii Vokzal, go in the door at the base of track 5, up the stairs, and wait in the lines at windows 15–20 (marked Суточная Продажа). For same-day tickets at Varshavskii Vokzal, visit window 2 in the main hall, marked "Intourist" (daily 8:00–11:30, 11:45–14:45, 15:45–17:30, 17:45–20:15, 21:00–23:00). Trains to Helsinki are a happy exception to this unpleasant procedure.

St. Petersburg to Helsinki: The Finnish-run *Sibelius* afternoon train is far more convenient than the Russian *Repin*. It's sleek, blue, and comfortable, and you can just hop on board and pay the conductor with a credit card, or in dollars or Finnish marks (although it's preferable, and slightly cheaper, to come a little early and buy a ticket at window 53 in the station). Since the *Sibelius* arrives in Helsinki in the evening, you should try to set up a place to stay by phone from St. Petersburg.

The Russian-run *Repin* is not as nice as the *Sibelius* (the price is the same). Since it leaves before the ticket windows open in the morning and since you can't pay on board, you have to buy your ticket the day before or earlier.

You can buy tickets for both trains from special windows at Finlyandskii Station itself, either in advance or on the day of departure. Walk two car-lengths up platform 1 and go in the door where you see an airplane symbol. Window 46 sells tickets for the Russian train. Next to 46, window 53 sells tickets for the Finnish train (both windows open Monday–Saturday 8:00–13:00 and 14:00–19:00, Sunday 8:00–13:00 and 14:00–16:00). As tickets on these trains almost never sell out, it's enough to come the day of departure (for the Finnish train) or the day before (for the Russian train). If you prefer, you can also get tickets for these trains at the Central Railway Booking Office, window 94 (not on the day of departure, though).

St. Petersburg to Poland: There are daily direct trains from St. Petersburg to Warsaw and Berlin, but since these transit Latvia, Lithuania, and then Belarus before Poland, you can't take them unless you have a Latvian visa (and Lithuanian for Canadians). Get to Poland instead from Moscow.

By Bus

St. Petersburg to Helsinki: The **St. Petersburg Express Bus** leaves St. Petersburg at 8:45 and arrives in Helsinki at 15:30—pick-ups at 8:00 at the Hotel Pulkovskaya near Metro: Moskovskaya, and 8:25 at Hotel Astoria (across from St. Isaac's), and 8:40 at Grand Hotel Europe. Make reservations at the Sovauto desk in the lobby of the Pulkovskaya (tel. 264-5125). The bus continues from Helsinki to Turku port, meeting the Turku–Stockholm overnight ferries. Tickets cost about $55, students $50 (to Turku, $70 and $62).

Pietarin Linja: St. Petersburg 12:00–Helsinki 19:35; no advance booking office, just buy tickets from the driver; departing daily from Hotel Moskva (Metro: pl. Aleksandra Nevskovo) at 12:00 and from the Hotel Astoria at 12:30. Tickets $41, students $37.

Finnord: St. Petersburg 15:30–Helsinki 22:00, handy English-speaking office and waiting room in St. Petersburg, departs from ul. Italyanskaya/Итальянская 37 (a half-block in from the Fontanka canal and a block from Nevsky Prospekt, Metro: Gostinii Dvor/Гостиныи Двор, tel. 314 8951, fax 314 7058 for reservations). Tickets $52, students $37.

St. Petersburg to Tallinn: Buses leave nightly at 22:45 from platform 5 at Bus Station #2, nab. Obvodnovo anala/Обводного Канала 36. Exit Metro: Ligovskii Prospekt/Лиговский Проспект, then go one tram stop south (just across the canal), and a block-and-a-half east along the canal. The bus arrives in Tallinn at 6:25 the next morning. Tickets $6.50.

By Boat

St. Petersburg to Stockholm and Helsinki: Baltic Line ferries run from St. Petersburg to Stockholm two times every week: departures on Wednesday and Sunday at 18:00, arrive at 17:00 the following day in Nynashamm (free connecting bus to Stockholm, 1.5 hrs). The port is not central so take the free Baltic Line/Commodore Hotel shuttle buses that leave every hour on the half-hour from the Catherine the Great monument on pl. Ostrovskovo along Nevsky Prospekt, steps from Metro: Gostinii Dvor/Гостиный Двор.

Baltic Line boats to Helsinki depart from St. Petersburg on Thursdays and Sundays at five minutes past midnight and

arrive at Helsinki's Makasiiniterminaali on Thursdays and
Sundays at 11:00. (See Helsinki section in Gateways chapter
for more information.)

The Baltic Line office on the second floor of the ferry
terminal (Monday–Friday 11:00–16:00 and sometimes later,
tel. 355-1616 or 355-1392) cannot give price information or
book tickets. Book your ticket abroad (if necessary by phone
from St. Petersburg). Call Baltic Line in Sweden at
46/8/5206 6600 or Finland at 358/0/651 011 with your credit
card handy, and you can just pick up your tickets a couple of
hours before you depart.

By Air

St. Petersburg's Pulkovo airport has two terminals: Pulkovo-I
handles domestic flights; Pulkovo-II, international flights.
To reach either, first take the Metro to the Moskovskaya/
Московская station, take the exit on the outbound end of the
station, and go all the way through the underground tunnel.
This will bring you out next to the stops for bus #13 (which
goes to Pulkovo-II) and bus #39 (which goes to Pulkovo-I). At
peak times bus #13 runs every 20 minutes. Since Pulkovo-II is
not the end of bus #13's route, there are both inbound and
outbound bus stops at the airport (marked by yellow signs).
If you have just landed and need to take the bus into town,
stand at the inbound stop (nearer the arrivals hall).

For tickets, you can visit major airlines' downtown offices
such as: **British Airways**, Nevsky Prospekt 57, tel. 119-6222;
Delta, ul. Gertsena (now Bolshaya Morskaya) 36, tel. 311-
5819; **Finnair**, ul. Gogolya (now Malaya Morskaya) 19, tel.
315-9736; **LOT**, ul. Karavannaya 1, tel. 272-2982; **Malev**,
Voznesenskii pr. 7, tel. 315-5455; **SAS, Swissair**, and
Austrian Air, Nevsky Prospekt 57, tel. 314-5086 or 311-6112.

TALLINN, ESTONIA

Tallinn is the flagship of Baltic reform. During the Soviet era, Tallinners spent their evenings watching Finnish television beamed across the gulf from Helsinki. When independence came, they knew exactly what a Western economy should look like. Since 1991 they've been putting one together as fast as possible. If only everyone in the ex-Soviet Union could learn from the Estonians.

Walk into any grocery store and you'll begin to understand. Tallinn has embraced the idea of the supermarket, where you pick food off the shelves yourself instead of asking clerks behind a counter to do it. The healthiest sign is that stores carry a sensible mix of imported and domestic goods, just like any other store in Europe. Estonian design has recovered from Sovietism: colorful, simple, Scandinavian layout is showing up in airline ads, yogurt packaging, and monthly bus-pass design. And Estonia's competitive trade policy is producing competitive goods: while Russian exports to Estonia have sunk, in Moscow you can now pick up Estonian orange juice, cucumbers, and frozen fish. This little country is succeeding.

Why the economic precociousness? One main reason is that Estonians consider their country a Nordic nation of solid, hardworking Protestant folk like those who made Scandinavia a showcase of order, propriety, and comfort. They're quick to point out that Finland and Estonia both gained independence from Russia after World War I, that as late as 1938, Estonia's living standard was equal to Finland's, and that Estonians would have kept pace had it not been for a couple hundred Russian tanks.

Of course, well-stocked grocery stores look perfectly normal if you come to Tallinn on the boat from Helsinki. This is why I suggest that you arrive in Tallinn from Russia or one of the other Baltic capitals. You'll feel like you're back in the West already. Coming from Helsinki, Tallinn looks run-down. Remember that it gets worse, and enjoy Tallinn while you can.

Estonians may dream of being the Hong Kong of the North, but others worry that Tallinn will become the Belfast of the Baltic. Russians were encouraged to settle in Estonia during the Soviet period. They now make up roughly a third of Estonia's population, though they are concentrated in very distinct areas. Most Russians don't want to leave; life in Estonia is better than life in their homeland. But laws passed since independence now require Russians living in Estonia to pass an Estonian language test in order to keep certain jobs, or to gain Estonian citizenship. The Russian government, pushed to the wall by nationalist pressures, has protested strongly. Estonia counters, among other arguments, that European and international observers have evaluated its ethnic policy favorably, and call attention to Russia's treatment of Estonians in areas that Russia seized from Estonia after World War II.

It is impossible to do justice to the issue here. Anatol Lieven discusses the problem of the Baltic Russians thoroughly and evenhandedly in his book *The Baltic Revolution*. As a traveler, you may sense that the issue gets blown out of proportion. You will see very little Russian-Estonian friction, most of the service personnel in stores in Tallinn seem to switch effortlessly and naturally from one language to the next, and Estonia's ethnic problems pale in comparison to the situation in Latvia.

Estonia's awkward demographics unfortunately allow for no clear imperatives. If Russians had moved into Estonia any earlier, few people alive would remember an Estonia without them. If they had come any later, there would be no Estonian-born Russian adults, and it would be easier to argue that Russians are occupiers who should go home. Similarly, if there were any more Russians in Estonia (like, say, in Latvia), on practical grounds Estonia would be forced to accommodate them more generously. If there were any fewer Russians (like, say, in Lithuania), their numbers might be small enough to assimilate.

But perhaps the most important point in the Russo-Baltic debate is that regardless of their citizenship, residents of the Baltics enjoy clean streets, well-stocked grocery stores, stable currencies, and a far better standard of living than those in Russia. The improvement in the Baltics is a direct result of the end of Russian and Soviet domination. And ultimately, economic health is probably a prerequisite for a generous resolution of the Baltic states' ethnic questions. Estonians must be puzzled to see that in most of Finland, with a Swedish population of only 6 percent, all public signs and services are bilingual. Estonia, with a Russian population of over 30 percent, is in full retreat from bilingualism. The difference, of course, is that Sweden is no longer an aggressive colonizing nation, while Finns have a sense of prosperity and national security that overshadows any "threat" from the Swedes in their midst. One can only hope that Estonia's future will be equally as calm.

Planning Your Time
Tallinn deserves more time than Riga or Vilnius. But it's fairly small and its sights are modest. On a first trip, two days are plenty.

Day 1
11:00 Wander through the Old Town, looking out for concert posters on your way up to Toompea, Tallinn's fortified hill.
12:30 Leisurely lunch at Toomkooli.
14:00 Go down to Kiek in de Kök and see the photography exhibitions.
15:00 Explore the small galleries and shops in the Old Town. Stop in any café when you want a rest.
19:00 Concerts usually take place at this time. Come a little early for tickets.
20:30 Dinner at Ai Sha Ni Ya.
22:00 Retire to Hell Hunt or the Eesli Tall cellar bar.

Day 2
10:00 Check out the Holy Ghost Church and perhaps the Tallinn Town Museum or the Estonian History Museum.
12:00 Assemble picnic fixings at the Kaubahall supermarket. Take the tram out to Kadriorg.
13:30 Picnic and walk through the Kadriorg park and palace grounds.
18:00 Return to the Old Town for dinner at Eesli Tall.
20:00 Plenty of time for mulled wine at the Virgin Tower, or a night train to Riga or St. Petersburg.

Tallinn Old Town

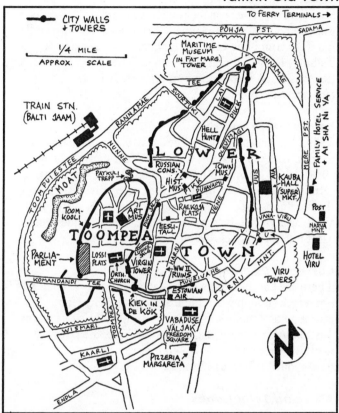

Orientation
(tel. code: 3722; tel. code within Baltics and Russia: 80142)

Tallinn owes its existence to Toompea, the precipitous hill on which the city's Upper Town stands. Fortified by the Danes after they captured Tallinn in 1219, Toompea turned into Tallinn's aristocratic neighborhood during the later Middle Ages—Toompea Castle still houses the Estonian government. Merchants and artisans, meanwhile, built the other half of old Tallinn, the Lower Town, beneath Toompea. Two steep, narrow streets—the "Long Leg" (Pikk jalg) and the "Short Leg" (Lühike jalg)—connect the two towns. Tallinn's intact city wall counts 29 watchtowers, each topped by a pointy red roof. Nineteenth- and early 20th-century architects circled the Old

Town, putting up broad streets of public buildings, low Scandinavian-style apartment buildings, and single-family wooden houses. Soviet planners then ringed this with endless stands of crumbling concrete high-rises where many of Tallinn's Russian immigrants settled. The Town Hall Square (Raekoja plats), in the center of the Lower Town, is an important reference point.

Tourist Information
Tallinn's excellent, English-speaking tourist office (on the main square, tel. 666 959, 9:00–18:00, Saturday–Sunday 10:00–16:00; closing an hour early off-season) has maps, concert listings, booklets, phrase books, postcards, free copies of the brochures *See Tallinn on Foot* and *Tallinn by Night*. Hotel Viru has a tour desk with maps that can answer questions. Most museums are closed on Mondays.

Currency Exchange
There are booths everywhere. Rates are pretty similar, so it's not worth shopping around extensively. Many larger exchange desks take traveler's checks with little or no commission. At major hotels, such as the Viru, the rates are notably worse and there is a commission on traveler's checks. $1 = about 11 Estonian kroons.

Mail and Telephones
Both services are in the fortresslike building across Narva mnt. from the Hotel Viru. Send letters from the second-floor post office (Monday–Friday 8:00–20:00, Saturday 9:00–17:00). For long-distance calls, the office on the lower floor of the post office building is open daily from 7:00–22:00. The best way to call is with a card that they sell in A (30kr), B (50kr), and C (100kr) sizes and that works in orange card phones in some of the booths. Calls to Helsinki, Riga, and Vilnius cost 5kr per minute; to Moscow, 6.5kr per minute; to Sweden, 7.5kr; to America, 24kr. Tallinn's pay phones take a 20-santim coin.

Helpful Hints
The **American embassy** is at Kentmanni tn. 20, third floor (tel. 312 021). **Seebimull Pesumaja**, a self-service and drop-off laundromat, is at Liivaliaia 7 (at the intersection with

Suda, tel. 682 010). **Lexicon**, on Vene 20, carries books exclusively in German and English. It doesn't have a very big selection, but it's worth visiting (Monday–Friday 10:00–18:00, Saturday–Sunday 10:00–15:00).

Getting Around Tallinn

Unless you're sleeping far from the center, you should be able to do most of your sightseeing on foot. Tallinn's trams are very simple and convenient. Check the map for route and stop locations. All trams meet in the center, by the Hotel Viru. The easiest way to get around Tallinn is to spend a couple of dollars on a ten-day card *(10-päeva-kaart)* which gives you unlimited rides on all public transport in Tallinn. You can also get single tickets. Cards and tickets are sold at the kiosks by tram stops that say *sõidutalongid* in the window. (There's a convenient one across from the Pinguin ice-cream parlor at the train station.) Taxis are cheap and handy in Tallinn. Fares in Ladas and Skodas are usually cheaper than in Mercedes or Toyotas.

Tallinn

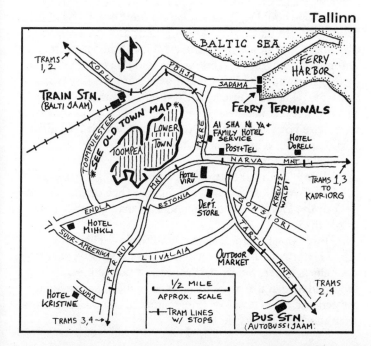

Sights—Tallinn

Tallinn has no incredible sights which demand to be seen. Rather, it steadily delivers small and pleasing towers, museums, ramparts, facades, churches, and shops. Wander through the Old Town, duck down every street and into every shop that looks interesting, and peer up at the Hanseatic facades and medieval towers.

▲▲▲**Toompea**—This is the fortified hill where Tallinn was founded in the 13th century and the Upper Town was built. Walk up Nunne tn., the street that leads from the train station to the Old Town, then cut off to the right and climb up the stairs. The ramparts at the top reward you with a perfect photo opportunity of the Lower Town's red roofs and steeples. Wandering will bring you to the **Dome Church** (Toomkirik) and eventually out to the square by the colorful **Russian Orthodox Church,** a plump, out-of-place, onion-domed edifice planted here after the Russian takeover of Tallinn in 1710. The interior is worth a peek.

Downhill from the church you'll see two towers. The square **Virgin Tower** (Neitsitorn) houses a café; the round one is **Kiek in de Kök** ("Peek in the Kitchen"), so named because one could supposedly spy on the Lower Town's residents from its heights. The top floor and the bottom two floors now house changing exhibits of the latest in Estonian photography, while in the middle you can see medieval cannons and charts left over from the Livonian wars (5kr, Tuesday–Friday 10:30–17:30, Saturday–Sunday 11:00–16:30). If you head back down to the Lower Town from here you'll pass by **St. Nicholas's Church** (Niguliste Kirik) and the World War II ruins behind it, left untouched as a memorial.

▲**Walking Tour**—You can hire a private walking tour of the Old Town. Just drop by the tourist office or the service desk in the Hotel Viru, or telephone Maila Saur at 650 975 or 650 873.

▲▲**Holy Ghost Church** (Pühavaimu Kirik)—This quintessentially northern 14th-century church has a fantastic old outdoor clock. Inside, hunched, whitewashed walls contrast with the faded medieval artwork on aged pews and galleries. Watch for periodic organ concerts. (Pühavaimu tn. and Pikk tn. across from the Maiasmokk café.)

▲**Estonian History Museum** (Eesti Ajaloomuuseum)—
Quite varied exhibits, so you may be able to find something
to hold your interest among archaeology, military history,
a roomful of domestic displays, and more. Look for the
English captions on the sides of the glass cases. The building is Tallinn's 15th-century Great Guildhall (2kr,
Thursday–Tuesday 11:00–18:00, Pikk tn. 17, across from
the Holy Ghost Church).

▲**Estonian Maritime Museum** (Eesti Meremuuseum)—
Housed in the Paks Margareta ("Fat Margaret") tower, the
museum itself is less interesting than the view of Tallinn's port
if you go out the wooden door on the top floor and up to the
tower roof. It's scary to think that anyone might have ever
used the suit of copper diving armor, built by a Tallinner in
the 1920s, that stands in a corner of the bottom floor (2kr,
Wednesday–Sunday, 10:00–18:00, Pikk tn. 70).

▲**Estonian Art Museum** (Eesti Kunstimuuseum)—Shouldn't
be your first stop in town, but if you're interested in late 19th-
and early 20th-century art, go check out what the Estonians
were doing. There's also a small case of avant-garde book-
printing from the 1920s (7kr, Wednesday–Monday 11:00–
17:30, Kiriku plats 1, on Toompea).

▲**Tallinn Town Museum** (Tallinna Linnamuuseum)—
Features Tallinn history from 1700 to 1918, with the upstairs
exhibit on Tallinn from 1900 to 1917 the best part. The mixture of Russian, German, and Estonian reminds us that the
ethnic situation here was once even more complicated than it
now is. (4kr, Wednesday–Friday 10:30–17:30, Saturday–
Sunday 10:30–16:30, Vene tn. 17 at Pühavaimu tn.)

▲▲**Kadriorg**—This seaside park and summer residence was
built by Peter the Great for Catherine after Russia took over
Tallinn in 1710. The mansion is now the home of the president of Estonia. The park, which runs down to the sea to the
north, is the perfect spot for your picnic. Trams #1 and #3 go
east from the center of town to Kadriorg at the end of the
line. It's an easy ride out and back.

▲▲▲**Estonian Music**—Tallinn has one of the densest per-
capita schedules of Baroque, Renaissance, and choral music
performances in Northern Europe. Estonian choral music got
its first push from the long German Lutheran presence in
Tallinn, and then became intimately bound up with the

struggle for independence after the first Estonian Song
Festival in 1869 (which is still held every five years). Even outside of festival times, it's a rare week in which there aren't a
few performances in Tallinn's churches and concert halls,
advertised on posters around town ("Hortus Musicus" is the
name of Estonia's best-known Renaissance music performance
group). Tickets rarely cost more than 20kr. In most cases they
are available in advance from the ticket office *(kontserdipiletite
müük)* inside the big theater (Monday–Saturday 13:00–19:00)
at Estonia pst. 4 across the park from the Hotel Viru, and then
at the door starting an hour before the performance. Estonian
groups have made only a few recordings since the end of the
Soviet period, but the place to look for them is the record
shop at Kuninga tn. 4, near Raekoja plats (Monday–Friday
9:00–19:00, Saturday 9:00–17:00).

▲▲**Artwork, handicrafts, and shopping**—For sweaters and
woolens, try the little shop on the second floor of Lühike jalg 2
(Wednesday–Saturday 11:00–17:00); the sweaters in this shop
are tagged with the names of their knitters, and although
woolens are marketed as a typically Estonian craft, most of the
names are Russian. **Diele Gallerii**, at Vanaturu kael 3 just
below Raekoja plats, sells the best postcards in town, displays
some drawings by the postmodern Estonian graphic artist
Eduard Wiiralt (died 1953), and has some nice art for sale.
Also check out the **BogaPott** ceramics store on Toompea at
Pikk jalg 9, next to what must be the cleanest public bathrooms in the ex-Soviet Union. The **Tallinn Department
Store** (Tallinna Kaubamaja), behind the Hotel Viru, is a brim-
ming, colorful, three-floor complex with a good mixture of
foreign and domestic goods. If you're living in Russia, you'll
particularly enjoy shopping here (Monday–Friday 9:00–20:00,
Saturday 10:00–18:00).

Sleeping in Tallinn
**(11 kroons = $1, tel. code: 3722; tel. code
within Baltics and Russia: 80142)**

Respectable Hotels
Hotell Mihkli delivers actual respectability at the best rates
in town. This means newish furniture, functioning bathrooms, locked parking, a TV, phone, and nice writing desk

in every room, and a welcoming reception desk. Singles with breakfast cost 400kr, doubles 600kr (the nicest doubles cost 680kr). It's past the National Library a little outside the center, but not too far to walk. You can also take trolleybuses #2, #3, or #6; the hotel is by the "Koidu" stop (Endla tn. 23, tel. 453 704, fax 451 767).

Hotel Viru towers over Tallinn like a mighty Indian god, and if you want large-hotel prices and standards, you might as well stay here. Singles with breakfast go for 840kr and doubles for 1,430kr (tel. 301 311, fax 301 303).

Hotell Kristiine barely makes it into the "respectable" category. The rooms are standard-issue Soviet style on several floors of a taller building, well-kept but with older furniture, TVs, and telephones. Each room has a small, spartan private bathroom. The reception was reasonably well-organized and spoke English in February, and has put a new sign out front. Singles with bath and breakfast cost 260kr, doubles 420kr. Take tram #3 or #4 to the "Vineeri" stop at the corner of Pärnu mnt. and Luha tn.; the hotel is about 3 blocks down Luha tn. at #16 (tel. 682 000, fax 682 030).

Cheaper Hotels and Hostels
Hotell Dorell, which occupies former student dorms, has double rooms with a hall bath for 250kr, towels and linen provided. Not much English spoken. Only 25 beds, so might be full. Take tram line #1 or #3 to the "Kreutzwaldi" stop, just east of the city center along Narva mnt. When you get off the tram, go through the archway at Narva mnt. 23 and you'll see the hotel sign to your left (Karu tn. 39, tel. 435 560).

The Barn—Centrally located one block off the town square, the Barn offers clean, bare-bones beds in dorm rooms for about $10. There are 16 spots for women, 36 for men, hot showers, plenty of common space, and a cozy little bar downstairs. Everyone speaks English (Vene 2, tel. 631 853).

Kuramaa tn. 15 is a way from town, but an option if everything else is full. These folks rent out entire two- and three-bedroom apartments in this building for short-term or long-term stays. The nicer apartments (which sleep four to six) go for 75kr per person, 65kr if you have a youth hostel card. Take bus #19 or #44 from the beginning of its route (the "Teenindusmaja" stop across the parking lot from the

Hotel Viru, in front of the Lembitukaubamaja) to its final turnaround point (a parking lot about 15 –20 minutes out into the suburbs). From there, Kuramaa tn. is the first cross-street as you walk into the apartment blocks, but bring a map, especially after dark. Go into the courtyard of #15 and in the door under the "Eesti Puhkemajad" sign; the office is in room 14B (tel. 327 781).

The **Hotell Kungla**, historically a cheap, somewhat seedy place, seems to be trying; the bathroom I saw had new tiling and fixtures and the receptionist spoke English. Still, this towering 160-room hotel is not a first choice. Doubles with private bath and breakfast cost 500kr; single occupancy costs 400kr. The hotel is at Kreutzwaldi tn. 23, at the corner of Gonsiori tn. (tel. 305 305, fax 305 315); you can reach it on bus #22 from the airport or the train station.

Hotel Nepi (DB-$50, Nepi 10, EE0013 Tallinn, tel. 655-1665, fax 655-1664) is a small, friendly, family-run hotel a short bus ride from the old town. They can pick travelers up at the station or airport with advance notice.

Private Rooms

Family Hotel Service rents out rooms in private homes without breakfast; singles run 106kr–178kr, doubles 170–292kr. Rooms in the Old Town cost most, medium-price rooms are usually a few minutes away by tram, while the cheapest rooms are a fair bus ride from the center. You can call the office (tel. 441 187) before you get to Tallinn, or you can just show up (daily 10:00–17:30, Mere puiestee 6, around the corner from the Hotel Viru; follow the signs up the driveway by the Chinese restaurant, and go in the building across the lot to the left).

CDS Reisid rents rooms in private homes (breakfast included) for a little more than the Family Hotel Service: singles 295kr, doubles 445kr. If you reserve ahead, they will also pick you up at the train station, ferry port, or airport. (Monday–Friday 10:00–18:00, Saturday–Sunday 10:00–15:00; mid-September to mid-May Monday–Friday 10:00–16:00, Raekoja plats 17, second floor, above the Kangur shop, tel. 445 262, fax 313 666.)

Rasastra is convenient for those arriving by sea. This office is just up the street, on the right, as you exit the ferry terminal. Singles cost 145kr–210kr, doubles 200kr–320kr, depending on location. No breakfast. (Daily 10:00–18:00, Sadama tn. 11, tel. 602 091.)

Eating in Tallinn

It's easy to get a good meal for $5 in Tallinn. It's hard to make it Estonian, though: the best restaurants are Chinese, Mexican, Italian, Indian, or vaguely international. Estonian cuisine is a bland, northern mixture of meat, potatoes, root vegetables, and soups, with some seafood now and then. Estonia's Saku beer, on the other hand, has an excellent reputation. Saku Originaal is the most widely drunk, but some prefer darker Saku Tume. You can also order local Värska mineral water for about 5kr–7kr a bottle. It's the best quality mineral water in the Baltics, but too salty to compete with imports.

Eesli Tall—There are now other restaurants in Tallinn with better menus and service, but few can match Eesli Tall ("Donkey Stable") for reliability and convenience (Sunday–Thursday 11:00–24:00, Friday–Saturday 11:00–1:00, Dunkri tn. 4/6, just uphill from the Town Hall). Everyone goes there, and so will you—expect crowds on summer weekends. The atmosphere in the restaurant is soothing and candlelit, and there are vegetarian options on the menu. Locals come not to the restaurant but to the perenially popular downstairs bar. Dungeon-walled, whitewashed, and bathed in colored lights, it's a maze of tunnels, archways, and hidden rooms. You can swirl with the lights by the bar and the band, or retreat into a quiet nook to talk. Saku (Estonian beer) goes for 15kr. (Daily 18:00–4:00, music 10:00–1:30, cover: 20kr after 19:00, tel. 448 033.)

Toomkooli is a modern restaurant which serves the best square meal on Toompea at fair prices (most entrees 30kr–90kr). The menu snubs the Scandinavians with a translation in English and German only, which seems vaguely appropriate for a selection heavy on meat, potatoes, mushrooms, and sausage. Consider reservations (daily 12:00–23:00, Toom-Kooli tn. 13, on the west edge of Toompea; AmEx, Visa, and MasterCard accepted; tel. 446 613).

Ai Sha Ni Ya is a real Chinese restaurant with reasonable prices, a relaxing atmosphere, and chopsticks on your table. Most of the dishes are bland because Estonians aren't used to spicy food (daily 12:00–23:00, Mere pst. 6, up a driveway from the street in the same courtyard as the Family Hotel Service, tel. 441 997).

Peetri Pizza is a chain with several branches in Tallinn and franchises elsewhere in Estonia. The Francescana is good (26kr per one-person pizza). The branch at Kopli tn. 2c (enter from Vana-Kalamaja tn.) is right by the train station, in the building on the corner across from the tram stop (daily, 11:00–22:00). The branch on Lai tn. 4 has only six seats but is just steps from the Town Hall Square (10:00–20:00), while the take-out-only branch by the tram stop at Pärnu maantee 22, between the advance bus ticket office and the Palace Hotel, is open from 10:00 to 3:00 in the morning (weather dependent), and takes phone orders at 666 711.

Pizzeria Margareta has decent pizzas for 35kr–50kr and is a much nicer place to sit than Peetri Pizza, although the crusts are disappointingly limp (daily 11:00–23:00, Pärnu mnt. 3, in the Palace Hotel at Vabaduse väljak; AmEx, Visa, and MasterCard accepted).

The Tex-Mex place (a.k.a. Foster's), at Tartu mnt. 50, is inside the Flexer Spordiklubi. It's hard to find (no one calls it by its official name and it doesn't have a sign) but worth the effort; serves barbecued meats of various sorts, tacos, the excellent "California burrito" for 35kr, and apple pie. From the center of town, either take tram #4 to the "Keskturg" stop and walk a little farther, or continue to the "Auto-bussijaam" (bus station) stop and walk back to Tartu mnt. 50 (Monday–Friday 9:00–21:00, Saturday–Sunday 10:00–21:00).

Restko—Try the *sel janka* (soup) at this excellent restaurant (31 Lai; head up to Hell Hunt, take first left, then first right, Restko is on the left in a cellar).

Hõbekass is Tallinn's best café to linger and talk in. There are plenty of tables in two rooms, with decent pastries and light meals (Monday–Friday 8:00–22:00, Saturday–Sunday 10:00–22:00, Harju tn. 7, near the World War II ruins).

For the best pastries in Tallinn, stop at the shop on the west side of the **Hotel Viru** complex, next to Stockmann's. Look for the "Kohvik" sign (take-out only; Monday–Friday

8:00–20:00, Saturday 9:00–20:00, Sunday 9:00–16:00). The **Maiasmokk** café and pastry shop (founded in 1864) at Pikk tn. 16, across from the Russian embassy, is the grande dame of Tallinn cafés, and a tasty place for breakfast if you're staying at the Barn. The runner-up for the café with the best pastries is **Wiiralti Kohvik** on Vabaduse väljak.

For the café with the best view, try the **Neitsitorn** (Virgin Tower), the square, many-windowed tower next to Kiek in de Kök. The top two floors overlook the Lower Town and serve hors d'oeuvres, pastries, and mineral water. In summer there's sometimes live classical music on the outdoor terrace. The bottom floor (go down the spiral staircase) and the ground level floor serve hot mulled wine *(hõõgvein)* out of wooden casks for 8kr per half-glass (daily 10:00–23:00, 3kr entrance fee after 16:00).

Hell Hunt is everyone's favorite hangout. The name of this Irish-style pub actually means Gentle Wolf in Estonian (Tuesday–Thursday 10:00–2:00, Friday–Saturday 10:00–3:00, Sunday–Monday 10:00–1:00, Pikk tn. 39). A more artsy crowd hangs out at the **Von Krahli** at Rataskaevu tn. 10.

For **picnic fixings**, just about every neighborhood in Tallinn now has a Western-style self-serve grocery store with an encouraging mixture of local and imported goods, like any other store in Europe. Among the biggest of these is the **Kaubahall**, a real supermarket, which opened in central Tallinn in the summer of 1993 (Monday–Saturday 9:00–20:30, Sunday 9:00–14:00, Aia tn. 7, not far from the twin Viru towers). The **Lembitukaubamaja**, across the bus lot from the Hotel Viru, is a smaller store open every day from 9:00 to 23:00.

Near Tallinn: Tartu and Saaremaa

The obvious day trip from Tallinn is to Tartu, Estonia's university town. Tartu's old city is built in a newer, classical style no less pleasing than Tallinn's Hanseatic center. Tartu has not managed Tallinn's commercial boom, although there is now a Peetri Pizza and a slew of Pinguin ice-cream parlors. You can put together a picnic at the Tartu Turg (market) in the center of town, then eat it on the banks of the Emajõgi River, which runs along the east side of the Old Town. Or head to the west, above the Old Town, to the set of bluffs where Tartu's ruined cathedral (partly rebuilt into an excellent museum) and early university buildings stand. The peeling paint of the 19th-century wooden houses that ring the old city, the ravines that cut through the bluffs, and the smell of coal-fired heating make parts of Tartu resemble a Massachusetts mill town.

Buses to Tartu leave roughly hourly from the Tallinn bus station between 6:00 and 21:00, take 3 hours, and cost 32kr one-way. You can also take a train, but it's less frequent and usually slower, and the train station is farther from the center of Tartu.

If you have time for a one- or two-night trip out of Tallinn and want to see the countryside, go to one of Estonia's big islands—Saaremaa or Hiiumaa. Buses take you from Tallinn to the coast at Virtsu, and then by ferry to Kuressaare, the main village on Saaremaa, in about 5 hours for 39kr. The Tallinn tourist office can give you advice on booking accommodations there.

Transportation Connections—Tallinn

By Train
The Tallinn train station (Balti jaam) is a short walk from the Old Town along Nunne tn. and a short, simple ride from the Hotel Viru by trams #1 or #2. This is the smallest, cleanest, and best-organized station in the Baltics, with few lines and fairly simple procedures. It has two parts: a smaller hall, at the head of the tracks, and a larger hall, which runs along the tracks.

In the small hall at the head of the tracks are **advance international ticket** purchase windows (numbers 7–12, under the *eelmüügi kassad* sign; Monday–Saturday 8:00–20:00, Sunday 9:00–17:00). Baltic Express tickets, however, must be purchased from a separate desk (see below). Across the room are the domestic ticket windows (same-day purchase only, from windows 15–18, under the *linnalähedaste rongide kassad* sign).

In the large hall along the tracks, there's a "left luggage" office (downstairs), currency exchange, an occasionally English-speaking *informatsioon* window, windows for purchasing tickets for **international trains leaving the same**

Trains Departing Tallinn

#	Destination	Departs	Arrives	2nd class	1st class
IK4	Moscow (Moskva)	18:06	10:50	340kr	697kr
K12*	▪	16:12	12:14	299kr	▪
K22	St. Petersburg (Peterburi)	23:05	8:51	148kr	299kr
R120	▪	20:10	6:11	158kr	▪
K10	Riga (Riia)	22:30	6:20	183kr	▪
IK2**	▪	17:40	0:05	271kr	▪
R100	▪	23:30	8:35	271kr	▪
K10	Vilnius	23:30	13:11	297kr	▪
8K	Warsaw (Varssavi)	17:40	14:42	567kr	875kr

*Slow train via Tartu.
**Baltic Express train.

day (windows 4–6, under the *ööpaeva kassad* sign), window 3 for returning tickets, and window 1 for processing phoned-in reservations (tel. 448 087 or 624 632). Upstairs, on the second floor, you'll find the Baltics Express desk, which reserves tickets for Estonian Railways' premier service, the **Baltic Express train** (Tallinn–Riga–Kaunas–Šeštokai–Warsaw). They give a 25 percent discount to students with an ISIC card.

With its own separate entrance door facing the platforms at the end of the larger hall, the Ageba Travel Agency sells plane tickets and some maps and guides, and speaks English (Monday–Saturday 8:00–20:00, Sunday 9:00–17:00).

There's also an Estonian Holidays office on the second floor of the Hotel Viru that will reserve train tickets but takes a commission of several dollars (daily 9:00–18:00, room 217). The Lufthansa City Center at Pärnu mnt. 10 (see By Air, below) can also issue train tickets. These agents are unfortunately not authorized to give the 25 percent Baltic Express student discount, which is available only at the station.

By Bus

Tallinn's bus station (Autobussijaam) is on Tartu maantee, a little too far from the center to walk comfortably; take tram

Buses Departing Tallinn

#	Destination	Departs	Arrives	Fare
90	Riga	8:15	13:35	69kr
40	"	12:45	18:55	96kr
40	"	15:00	21:05	96kr
40	"	23:40	5:40	96kr
949-2	Vilnius	21:30	9:20	154kr
970	St. Petersburg	7:30	15:20	98kr
970	"	16:00	23:50	98kr
-	Warsaw*	7:00	24:00	390kr

*Monday and Wednesday only.

#2 or #4 east from the city center to the "Autobussijaam"
stop. Most buses are run by the Estonian state company,
Mootor. You can buy tickets in advance at the Mootor
office (daily 8:00–19:00, Pärnu maantee 24, just past Peetri
Pizza) or at windows 1 and 2 in the station. On the day of
departure, you have to buy tickets at the station (windows
4–6). The international buses are all daily except the
Warsaw bus and all leave from platform 1.

By Boat
The ferry port in Tallinn is at the end of Sadama tn., a 20-
minute walk from the center of town. Bus #65 does a coun-
terclockwise circuit from the port to the train station,
Vabaduse väljak, the Hotel Viru, and back to the port; trams
#1 and #2 also stop 5 minutes from the terminals at the base
of Sadama tn. Unless you really have a lot of luggage, avoid
taking taxis, which will surely overcharge. As you approach
the port from town, the new Finnish Terminal (Soome terminaal, with boats to Helsinki) is on your left and the smaller Swedish Terminal (Rootsi terminaal, with boats to
Stockholm) is on your right.

See the Helsinki and Stockholm sections in the
Gateways chapter for full fare and schedule details on the
Tallink ferries to Helsinki and the Estline ferries to
Stockholm. Any travel agent in Tallinn will sell you a ferry
ticket, or you can get it direct from the companies (AmEx,
Visa, and MasterCard accepted).

Tallinn has a ticket office in the port (daily 9:00–19:30, tel. 601 960) and in the town (Monday–Saturday 9:00–18:00, Pärnu mnt. 16, tel. 442 440 or 602 822). Estline also has a ticket office in the port (daily 9:00–18:45, tel. 313 636, fax 425 352) and one in town (Monday–Friday 9:00–17:00, Aia tn. 5a, tel. 448 348).

By Air

Tallinn's airport is the best of the five cities in this book. Bus #22, which starts at the train station, passes through Vabaduse väljak and along Estonia pst. and Gonsiori tn. before terminating at the airport (runs every 20–30 minutes). The airport is quite close to town, and fair taxi drivers (who do exist) using the meter will charge no more than about 25kr to the center.

For tickets, visit the airport; the Estonian Air ticket office at Vabaduse väljak 10 (tel. 446 382); or the Lufthansa City Center office at Pärnu mnt. 10 (Monday–Friday 9:00–17:00, Saturday 10:00–15:00, tel. 444 037 or 449 917; fax 440 290), which handles the major Western airlines as well as Estonian Air and can book youth fares.

RIGA, LATVIA

Tall 19th- and 20th-century buildings give Riga a cosmopolitan feel and a vertical accent unique among the Baltic capitals. Bishop Albert of Bremen, German merchants, and the Teutonic Knights made Riga the center of Baltic Christianization, commercialization, and colonization when they founded the city in the early 1200s. Under the czars, the city was the Russian Empire's busiest commercial port. Under Soviet rule, Riga became first an important military center and later, because of its high standard of living, one of the favored places for high-ranking military officers to retire to (they were given a choice of anywhere in the U.S.S.R. except Moscow, Kiev, and St. Petersburg). The Soviets encouraged Russian immigration and the percentage of residents who were Latvian plunged from well over half to about a third today.

The result is that although all the street signs are now in Latvian only, life in Riga goes on in two languages. Lithuanian and Estonian dominate Vilnius and Tallinn despite large Russian populations, but in Riga you'll hear Russian on the street just as much as Latvian. Latvia's major newspapers, such as the daily *Diena*, come out in dual Russian and Latvian editions. And Lutheranism notwithstanding, Riga is the most Soviet-feeling Baltic capital city. It has not visibly Westernized itself as much as Tallinn; it still lacks supermarkets and a fleet of shiny airline offices. Still, Riga is far ahead of most of the ex-U.S.S.R. on the road to economic viability, and what it *has* done has muscle. The Latvian lat is the strongest currency in the Baltics. Some predict that Riga is on the verge of an economic boom that will outstrip Tallinn.

Riga's Old Town is the least medieval in the Baltics. The big churches, the moat, the bastion, fragments of the city walls, a couple dozen houses, and the cannonballs embedded in the Powder Tower are all that survive from the Middle Ages. Much of the Old Town is in 18th-century classical style; the rest of the center, and almost all of the newer parts that immediately ring it, are fine examples of late 19th- and early 20th-century building styles, particularly the Art

Nouveau that betrays Riga's connections to the German-speaking world. Emerging from the Soviet period, many of these buildings no longer have quite enough warmth and life to fill their once-elegant, high-ceilinged rooms. But they are still very nice to look at. The best way to do this is to walk along the streets near the parks (such as Elizabetes) and around the city's main commercial artery—Brīvības iela—which starts by the Freedom Monument and runs away from the Old Town and the Daugava River.

Planning Your Time
Like Tallinn, Riga is worth two days but, for most, no more. Here's how I'd spend them.

Day 1
10:00 Go up St. Peter's Church for a look around Riga.
12:00 Grab a sandwich at Fredis.
13:00 Learn your way around the Old Town, visiting the

Riga

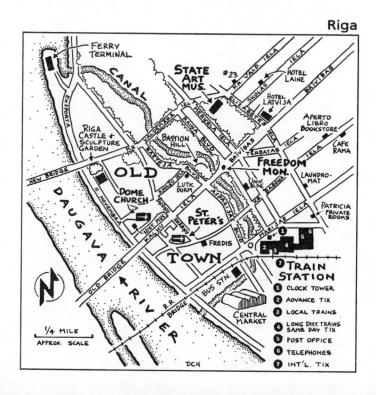

Dom and the Museum of the History of Riga, and buy
concert tickets if there's anything you want to hear.

18:00 Dinner at Zilais Putns.

Day 2

10:00 Explore Riga's central market.
12:00 Go to the Hare Krishna café for lunch.
14:00 Walk up to the Art Museum.
16:00 Extra time for another museum or another look
around the Old Town.
18:00 Dinner at Pie Kristapa, if it's still there.

Orientation
**(tel. code: 3712; tel. code within
Baltics and Russia: 80132)**

Riga's Old Town is on the right bank of the Daugava, which
is very wide and crossed by only two bridges. The bus and
train stations and most sights, shops, and services are either
in the Old Town or in the 19th-century section of town
immediately around it. You should never need to venture
across the river, unless you wind up sleeping there.

Tourist Information

Although people in Riga recognize the need for a central
tourist information office, the city and the national government are still bickering over who will pay for it and where
it will be. If you arrive at the airport, take advantage of the
info desks there. Otherwise, the Latvian Tourist Board
administrative offices at Pils laukums 4, second floor (near
the castle) have set aside one room as a public information
office, but they have very few brochures on display and
don't seem ready to cope with walk-in visitors (they're
only open Monday–Friday 9:00–18:00). The "Patricia"
room-finding service at Elizabetes iela 22 (see Sleeping,
below) advertises free tourist advice and does have a lot of
good information posted on their walls, but this is not what
they're in business for.

Buy the handy information booklet, *Riga in Your Pocket*,
at a kiosk or newsstand. The Riga-based newspaper, the
Baltic Observer, lists all events in English. The erratically
available *Riga This Week* is an option but is really too

encumbered with casino and nightclub ads to be worth buying. Pick up a Riga street map from a kiosk or the bookstores along Aspazijas bulv.

Currency Exchange

Everywhere. Rates are similar; try to find a place with no commission and a 1 percent spread between buying and selling rates. The **American Express** representative, Latvia Tours, cannot cash your checks but can replace lost checks and cards, hold client mail, issue checks against your card, and cash emergency checks (Monday–Friday 9:00–18:00, Grecinieku iela 22/24, fourth floor, in the Old Town, tel. 266 155 or 721-3627). Rīgas Komercbanka changes American Express checks for a commission of 1 percent or $5, whichever is higher (Monday–Friday 9:00–13:00 and 14:00–15:30, Smilšu iela 6, near the Dom). $1 = about 0.5 lats (Ls). 1 lat = 100 santims (s).

Mail and Telephones

The main post office is in an extension of the train station building. There is a main phone office catty-corner from the Freedom Monument at Brīvības iela 19 (open 24 hours) and a branch at the train station. Either will sell you the tokens you need for Latvian pay phones. Unfortunately, the Latvian telephone system is both the most expensive and the most difficult to use in the Baltics. Local calls demand single-slotted tokens, which cost 1s and give you 2 minutes within Riga. Long-distance phones take double-slotted tokens, which cost 6s and give you 3 minutes within Latvia or a few seconds to the other Baltics or Russia.

Helpful Hints

The **American embassy** is at Raiņa 7 (tel. 721-0005). **Aperto Libro** is an excellent English-language bookstore with especially friendly staff and a limited but well-selected stock including guidebooks, Baltic history, maps, fiction, textbooks, and dictionaries (Monday–Saturday 10:00–19:00, Kr. Barona iela 31, tel. 728-3810).

Laundry

The **Miele laundromat**, through the archway at Elizabetes iela 85a, is a savior for travelers in the Baltics. Two blocks from the train station, it has brand-new German machines and a café. Self-service costs 2.96 Ls per large load, full-service 4.72 Ls (daily 8:00–20:00, less busy on weekdays, tel. 721-7696).

Getting Around Riga

Tickets for Riga's buses, trams, and trolleybuses are sold at kiosks for 12s apiece. If you are staying in the center, you can walk almost everywhere. Taxi rides around the center of town should cost between 50s and 1 Ls.

Sights—Riga

▲▲▲**State Museum of Latvian Art** (Latvijas valsts mākslas muzejs)—This is the best art museum in the Baltics. The grand staircase is impressive, but especially worthwhile is the permanent exhibition of Latvian art on the second floor. The collection, almost entirely from 1910–1940, concentrates all the artistic and political influences that stirred Latvia then: French impressionism, German design, and Russian propaganda-poster style on the one hand; European internationalism, Latvian nationalism, rural romanticism, and Communism on the other. Check out the Russian art on the first floor if you won't make it to St. Petersburg (Monday and Wednesday–Friday 11:00–17:00, Saturday–Sunday 11:00–18:00, Oct.–Mar. Wednesday–Monday 11:00–17:00; Kr. Valdemāra iela 10).

▲▲**Freedom Monument** (Brīvības piemniekelis)— Dedicated in 1935, located on a traffic island in the middle of Brīvības iela, this monument was strangely left standing by the Soviets. KGB agents, however, apprehended anyone who tried to come near it. Now it is again the symbol of independent Latvia, and locals lay flowers between the two soldiers (wearing Latvian army uniforms from the inter-war period) who stand guard at the monument base.

▲▲**St. Peter's Church** (Pētera baznīca)—St. Peter's distinctive wooden spire, which used to be the tallest structure in Riga, burned down during World War II. The present steel replica was built during the Soviet period. Take the elevator up to the observation deck for 1 lat. You can visit the inside of the church afterwards for 20s (Tuesday–Sunday 10:00–19:00, Sept.–April 10:00–17:00; in the Old Town).

▲▲**Riga Dom** (Doma baznīca)—Also in the Old Town, Riga's most formidable church dates from 1211. You can go inside for 30s (Tuesday–Friday 13:00–16:00, Saturday 10:00–14:00). The inscriptions recall Latvia's German Lutheran heritage, and in fact the crypt holds what's left of Bishop Albert of Bremen, who started it all. The Dom has a first-class organ and often hosts good choirs; concert tickets (usually under 1 lat) are available at the ticket office at Riharda Vāgnera iela 4 or downstairs in the Filharmonic building at Amatu iela 6 (both a few blocks away and open daily 12:00–15:00 and 16:00–19:00). Just down the street from the Dom toward the river is a statue of the philosopher Johann Gottfried Herder, born in Riga in 1744, whose influential writings on nationalism were partly shaped by growing up among the Balts.

▲▲**Museum of the History of Riga and Navigation** (Rīgas vēstures un kugniecības muzejs)—Although there are only a few English labels, this large exhibit gives a fairly good idea of Riga's early history as a center on the Baltic–Black Sea trade route, explains the Old Town's street plan in terms of a now-silted-up river that used to flow through the center, and shows you everything you wanted to see on inter-war Riga. If you like it, you'll probably want to spend several hours exploring (30s, Wednesday–Sunday 11:00–17:00, Palasta iela 4, behind the Dom).

▲▲**Central Market** (Centrālais tirgus)—This is the most accessible central market in all of the Baltics and gives you a real insight into life here. It sprawls in and around the large former Zeppelin hangars between the train station and the river (go under the tracks).

▲▲**Other Attractions**—If you have more time, check out the Museum of Decorative Arts (Dekoratīvi lietikās mākslas muzejs) at Skārnu iela 10/20; the Motor Museum (Motormuzejs) on S. Eizenšteina iela in suburban Riga, which houses the cars of Soviet leaders, including Stalin's (take bus #21 along Brīvības iela); or even farther out, in good weather, the Open-Air Ethnographic Museum (Etnogrāfiskais brīvdabas muzejs), which shows farm buildings from all over Latvia (take bus #1 or #9 along Brīvības iela to the first stop across the bridge over Lake Jugla).

Sleeping in Riga
(1 lat = about $2, tel. code: 3712; tel. code within Baltics and Russia: 80132)

Hotels and Hostels
Hotel Rīdzene is central, fairly modern, and professional, but like so many expensive hotels it gives only a little more value than somewhere like Hotel Laine. It's perhaps the best choice in its price range, though: in contrast to some of the Rīdzene's competitors the lobby is free of casino advertisements, thuggish young men in security uniforms, outdated ferry brochures, and likely prostitutes. Singles 77 Ls, twin-bed doubles 85 Ls, breakfast included (R. Endrupa iela 1, Visa and MasterCard accepted, tel. 324 433 or 733-4498, fax 324 422).

Krišjāņa Valdemāra 23, formerly a closed hotel for Supreme Soviet deputies, is now under new management. It has shabby dignity—the bathrooms need a little work and the furniture is very old—but the place retains some order and civility; sweaty backpackers will feel underdressed and should stay elsewhere. Doubles with bath cost 25 Ls–30 Ls; singles are also available (Kr. Valdemāra iela 23, catty-corner from the State Museum of Latvian Art, tel. 733-2132).

Hotel Laine, the former home of Riga's American Peace Corps volunteers, has been remodeled, and the facilities are bright and clean. Two singles cost 9 Ls each, two doubles 14 Ls, five triples 18 Ls, one quad 20 Ls (all with hall bath). Seven doubles with private baths cost 21 Ls. The hotel will serve you breakfast for one lat. You can walk from the train station or the Old Town, but coming from the station with a lot of luggage, cross the street and take trolleybus #3 from the stop on Merķeļa iela for three stops; this will leave you on Kr. Valdemāra iela around the block from the hotel. At Skolas iela 11, look for the "Laine" sign, go into the courtyard, in the door on the far left, and up to the reception on the fourth floor (tel. 728-8816, also 728-7658, which becomes a fax after business hours).

The Latvian University Tourist Club (LUTK) rents rooms in two student dormitories in Riga. In the dorm above the Europcar office at Basteja bulv. 10 (in the Old Town and within short walking distance of the train station, tel. 220

703), they rent by the bed in rooms with a hall bath (6 Ls per person), and have one single with bath (12 Ls) and one double with bath (20 Ls). They also have one floor of a less luxurious dormitory about 20 minutes from the center for only 3 Ls per night (Burtnieku iela 1b; take trolleybus #4 from the stop near the train station, get off at Aizkraukles iela, and walk about four blocks). *Note:* Even if you reserve ahead, you must go to the LUTK office before you go to the dormitories. Someone (usually English-speaking) is normally on duty there daily from 9:00 to at least 18:00 (Raiņa bulv. 19, room 107, tel. 225 298 or 228 320, fax +371 882-0113). The office is about two blocks from the Riga train station in the dark stone university building with a white thermometer on the right side of the main door. On weekends, ring the bell or call ahead. Room 107 is on the right side of the building's ground floor.

Hotel Viktorija—The staff's new uniforms and the remodeled lobby symbolize that this place is slightly above the other cheap hotels in town, but it's still dingy. The hotel has plenty of run-down but habitable doubles, with questionable toilets and showers down the hall, for 13 Ls to 20 Ls—a good deal for student backpackers. Doubles with bath start at 10 Ls and range up to 46 Ls for some actually fairly nice corner suites (A. Čaka iela 55, tel. 272 305, fax 276 209). From the train station, the hotel is eight walkable blocks up Marijas iela (which turns into A. Čaka iela); you can also hop on trolleybus #11 or #22.

Youth hostels—The Latvian Youth Hostel Association recently opened an office at Minsterjas iela 8/10. It's not well marked; look for the institutional plaque for the Latvia Hospitality Institute near the entrance (Monday–Friday 9:00–18:00, in the Old Town a few blocks toward the river from the train station, tel. 225 307 and 721-0513). English-speaking staffers can book you a room in 16 different hostels across Latvia, including several in Riga.

Private Rooms
Patricia Ltd. speaks English and finds rooms for an average of $15 per person per night without breakfast. Entire apartments (minimum three nights' stay) cost $30–$50 per night. They also do sightseeing tours and provide guides. Call

ahead or stop by their office (daily 9:00–18:00; November–April Monday–Friday 9:00–18:00, Saturday and Sunday 9:00–13:00; Elizabetes iela 22-4a, very near the train station, tel. 728-4868, tel./fax 728-6650).

Latvian Tourist Club charges $15 per person per night in private homes without breakfast. In the same building as the office, they also have four double rooms with private washbasin but shared bath for $30–$50 per room per night (possible discounts in winter or for single occupancy). The location is fantastic; the rooms are acceptable (daily 9:00–18:00; October–April Monday–Friday 9:00–18:00; Skarnu iela 22 behind St. Peter's Church, tel. 223 113 or 221 731, fax 227 680). If you call, ask for Aira Andriksone, who speaks English. If you come by, go up the stairs to the second floor and knock on the first door to your right.

Eating in Riga

Fredis Café serves up small, tasty, slightly expensive sub sandwiches in the Old Town (0.75Ls–1.25 Ls, halves available). It's part of a bakery, so the bread's good. Seating is limited, but you can call ahead for larger take-out orders. Vegetarian options and English menus available (daily 9:00–24:00, Audēju iela 5, tel. 721-3731).

Zilais Putns has a sign outside that says "Picērija," but you can only get pizza at the downstairs bar. Upstairs is an elegant but not too expensive Italian restaurant with a view of part of the Dom Square and entrees in a very wide price range: from 2.5 Ls for simple but artfully prepared pasta dishes to 12.50 Ls for lobsters boiled in beer (daily 12:30–2:00, Tirgoņu iela 4, Visa and MasterCard accepted).

At **Rama**, filling Indian vegetarian food is dished out by, you guessed it, the International Society for Krishna Consciousness. They don't try to convert foreigners, and whatever you think of their beliefs, they do get credit for feeding a lot of hungry, impoverished Latvians and providing a place to recover from a week of fried cutlets. Full meals 70s–80s (Monday–Saturday 12:00–18:00, Kr. Barona iela 56; the café is through the front door of the building and to the left).

Don-Fa is a little dim and shabby on an absolute scale, but it's Riga's best value in Chinese food. Meals come in at

about 5 Ls. Fair selection of vegetarian entrees (daily
12:00–23:00, Avotu iela 33, at the corner of Gērtrudes iela;
from the train station, walk away from the river up Marija
iela, which turns into A. Čaka iela, and turn right on
Gērtrudes iela one block to Avotu iela).

Pie Kristapa is the last of the decent state-run restaurants and one of the best places to go for real Latvian food,
but the building has been privatized and the restaurant may
have to move. If it's gone, ask where to; if it's still there, go
downstairs, where you can order a 2.5-liter pitcher of beer
for 95s and *zirņi* (black peas with smoked fat) for 1.23 Ls or
sausage for 1.77 Ls (daily 12:00–18:00 and 19:00–24:00,
Jauniela 25/29, on the street that runs off the square from
the back end of the Dom).

Sigulda, a stand-up café at Brīvības iela and Merķeļa
iela, is nothing special, but has good pastries and opens at
8:00 (Saturday–Sunday at 9:00). The friendly **Kafenica Lita**
on Marijas has good coffee and pastries, **Pizza Lula** on
Veldemara is worth a taste, and the **café** in the bookstore at
Kr. Barona iela 31 is highly recommended.

For **picnic fixings**, go to the Central Market behind
the train station, or to the first floor of the Universālveikals
(department store) at Audēju iela 16.

Near Riga: Jūrmala and Valmiera

A sunny summer day might be the time to go to **Jūrmala**,
Riga's seaside resort. You can't swim (too polluted), but you
can set up a beach chair. Go to the local-trains waiting room
in the station; trains to Jūrmala are posted in red. Tickets to
Majori, the most popular section of Jūrmala, are available
from the windows in the same waiting room.

Other popular short trips are to towns like **Sigulda**,
Cēsis, and **Valmiera** along the Gauja River northeast of
Riga. The Latvian University Tourist Club (see Sleeping,
below) can fix you up a spot in one of their cabins at
Valmiera, about 2 hours by local train from Riga. The cabins are about 2.5 km from Valmiera station, sleep six, and
cost 12 Ls per night; food and hot showers are available
on-site. Canoeing, hiking, and biking are nearby and you
can catch the train to Tallinn from Valmiera if you're heading that way.

Transportation Connections—Riga

By Train

Riga's train station *(centrālā stacija)*, though not overly crowded, is confusing at first. See the map on page 99 for help. There are two main halls.

The long-distance train departure hall is #4 on our map. To one side of it are ticket windows (numbered 3–8) for trains leaving the same day; to the other side is the entrance to the tunnel to the platforms. If you go up the stairs (rather than through the tunnel) and outside, you get more quickly to platforms 1 and 2, where most long-distance trains leave from. If you go all the way through the tunnel, emerge outdoors on the other side of the tracks, and hang a right, you reach the international ticket office *(starptautiskās kases,* #7 on our map; Monday–Saturday 8:30–13:00 and 14:00–19:30, Sunday 8:30–13:00 and 14:00–17:30).

The local-train departure hall is #3 on our map. In its near right corner is a passage leading to the room with advance ticket sales windows for long-distance trains *(iepriekš pārdoš anas kases,* #2 on our map; the windows are numbered 25–34; Monday–Saturday 8:00–19:00, Sunday 8:00–18:00). Lines are fairly short. Come here at least 24 hours before your departure, preferably a couple days earlier. On your way, stop in the long-distance train departure hall (#4) by the information window *(uzziņu birojs)* and check the computer screen which lists ticket availability on major trains by number, destination, departure time, and date. It uses the Cyrillic letters Л, К, П, О, and С to indicate free space in first-class sleepers, second-class sleepers, third-class *(platskart)* sleepers, and the two varieties of seating-cars, respectively.

Some Comments on Trains

Train #2, the *Latvijas Ekspresis,* is Latvia's flagship. You can buy tickets only at windows 26 and 27 in the advance ticket office (#2 on our map; daily 8:00–18:00). Your ticket comes in a snazzy new airplane-style cover. On board, conductors provide newspapers, serve meals in your compartment, and are rumored to speak English. You can also watch videos. All this costs extra, of course, while the ride itself costs twice as much as train #4 but doesn't get you to Moscow any faster.

Trains Departing Riga

#	Destination	Departs	Arrives	2nd class	1st class
2	Moscow	17:40	11:00	20 Ls	40.5 Ls
4	"	18:30	12:20	"	"
38	St. Petersburg	19:25	8:16	16 Ls	25 Ls
187	Vilnius	6:40	23:23	8 Ls	-
221	"	22:15	6:30	"	-
13*	Warsaw**	00:25	8:05	22.5 Ls	-
14	Tallinn**	6:25	13:10	24 Ls	-
188	"	23:38	8:10	"	-

*Train for Warsaw is marked "Sestokai," where you change to the Polish train for Warsaw.

**Tickets available only at international windows.

Trains #13 and #14 are Estonia's flagship service, the Baltic Express, which you pick up in Riga on its way between Tallinn and Šeštokai, Lithuania, where it connects with the train to Warsaw. You must buy tickets at the international office (#7). See the Gateways chapter, Warsaw section, for more information on taking this train to Poland.

By Bus

Coming from the train station, Riga's bus station (*autoosta*) is on the other side of the tracks and a few minutes' walk past the central market towards the river. Buses to both Tallinn and Vilnius leave from platform 2; tickets can be bought at windows 2–8. Buses to Tallinn leave daily at 7:20, 11:50, 15:00, and 23:40, arriving at 14:00, 18:20, 23:40, and 6:05, respectively. Service to Vilnius (2.20 Ls) is overnight only, leaving at 20 minutes past midnight and arriving at 6:20 in the morning—take the train instead. A twice-weekly Tallinn–Warsaw bus stops in Riga on the way, leaving from *stance* 1 Monday and Thursday at 12:10; tickets cost $20 and are available from window 17.

In the bus station, a sign in front of the information window (#1) says in Latvian: "Questions, 2 santims. Complicated questions, 4 santims." Common in Soviet times, the notion that you must pay for information and that one can objectively tell the difference between a simple and a complicated question is almost gone in the Baltics and seems thankfully on the way out in Russia as well.

By Boat
The ferry port in Riga is a little north of the Old Town. You can walk, but it's easier to catch a cab or any of the trams that run along Aspazijas bulv. Several companies have run ferries to Sweden, Germany, and Denmark over the past few years, but schedules are unpredictable. The best way to find the latest information is to come to the offices in the port terminal during business hours.

By Air
Riga's airport (Lidosta Riga) has been remodeled into adequate working order. If you arrive after 17:00, when the government-funded information office on the arrivals level closes, go up to the second floor where there's a small information booth. If you take a taxi from (or to) the airport you will be ripped off; instead, buy three bus tickets (for zones 1–3, 4s each) and board bus #22, which runs between the airport and Arhitektu iela in the center of town (between the Freedom Monument and the train station).

In the city, you can get tickets for most airlines (including Latvian Airlines, Finnair, SAS, Baltic International Airlines, and Lufthansa, but not LOT or CSA, which must be purchased at the airport) at the Lufthansa City Center (Monday–Friday 9:00–18:00, Saturday and Sunday 10:00–14:00, Kr. Barona iela 7/9, tel. 728-5901 or 728-5614 fax 371/882-8199). SAS youth fares, however, can only be purchased at their airport office.

VILNIUS, LITHUANIA

Sprawling and disorganized, a Catholic church on every corner, Vilnius is the homiest and coziest of the three Baltic capitals, and also the most unsophisticated and run-down. A restful, horizontal city, Vilnius's one- and two-story buildings and its arches and courtyards are more reminiscent of a friendly Polish provincial capital than of the tall German-influenced architecture in Riga or the Hanseatic frosting-cake feel of Tallinn. No wonder, considering Lithuania's centuries-long political and religious ties with Poland, and the fact that Poland occupied Vilnius from 1920 to 1939 while most of the rest of Lithuania was independent.

Vilnius' Old Town (the buildings date largely from the 17th and 18th centuries) is huge and, unlike Riga's or Tallinn's, amazingly dilapidated: burned-out windows, crumbling wooden shutters, cracked plaster, and bowed roofs cry out for millions of dollars' worth of restoration work (while certain Soviet "improvements," like the central telephone office, cry out for the wrecking ball). The fact that Vilnius is falling apart gives the visitor a heightened sense of possibility. Every paneless window and paintless shutter makes you think of what could be there: a family, a shop, candles on the table, children in the street. Riga and Tallinn, in contrast, are much more accounted for.

Vilnius' disorganization also challenges you to explore. The Old Town is full of cozy cafés and fascinating galleries and shops, but you have to duck through archways into courtyards, open gates and doors, and slowly learn your way from nook to cranny. Some streets, such as Totorių g., transport you back to turn-of-the-century Eastern Europe, when Vilnius was an ethnic hodgepodge of Lithuanians, Poles, White Russians, and a booming Jewish community. These days Vilnius is half Lithuanian, half Polish and Russian, and all three languages are very much in evidence on the streets. Lithuania as a whole, however, is 80 percent Lithuanian and less than 10 percent Russian. Russian minority rights are not so big an issue here.

Paradoxically, while Lithuania is the Baltic state with the smallest Slavic population, it is the most Slavic in temperament and feel. Vilnius, as the only inland Baltic capital, was always politically and economically closer to Poland and Russia than to Scandinavia. Lithuania's president, Algirdas Brazauskas, is a former Gorbachev-era reform Communist. Lithuanian politics and society have the mildly theatrical quality that you see in Russia but not in Latvia or Estonia. And Vilnius certainly feels like more of a Soviet city than Tallinn—though this is not the harsh, urban Sovietism of Riga, but rather the provincial inertia that at the same time makes Vilnius endearing.

Planning Your Time

Day 1
11:00 Hike up Castle Hill and climb the tower.
13:00 Go into the Old Town for lunch at the Stikliai café.
14:00 Visit the Jewish Museum.
15:00 Wander through the Old Town and look into its
       churches, shops, and university.
18:00 Dinner at Medininkai.

Day 2
10:00 Visit the KGB Museum.
12:00 Lunch at Geležinis Vilkas or Literatų Svetainė.
14:00 Check out the Art Museum, the National Museum,
       or the State Museum across the river.
18:00 End your visit with dinner at the Turistas.

Orientation
**(tel. code: 3702; tel. code within the Baltics
and Russia: 80122)**
Vilnius' Old Town sprawls from the river and the cathedral all the way up to the train station. Walking from the station downhill to the river is pleasant. To reach the Old Town from the station, turn right and follow Geležinkelio g. down the hill along the train tracks, then turn left down Aušros Vartų g. where the tracks cross on an overpass. Go straight through the Aušros Vartai (Gates of Dawn) and keep heading downhill.

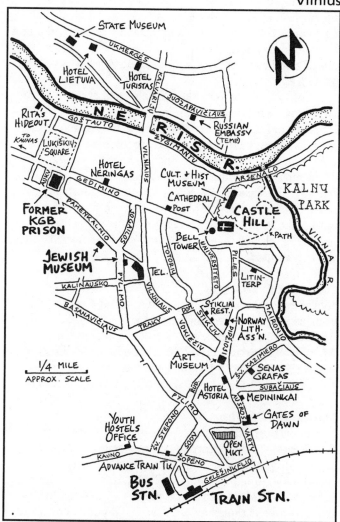

Vilnius

Tourist Information

Vilnius has no tourist office. It does, however, have an
incredibly good city guidebooklet called *Vilnius In Your
Pocket*, written by German journalist Matthias Lüfkens, and
on sale everywhere in town for 4 litas (Lt). As soon as you
arrive and change money, go to the nearest kiosk and buy it
for its wit, maps, trolleybus map, and feature stories. This

book can't possibly hope to better the comprehensive information in *VIYP*. I have, however, tried to save you having to mow through its masses of detail by selecting the best *few* restaurants, hotels, and sights. If you exhaust the restaurant or hotel choices that I've listed below, refer to *Vilnius In Your Pocket*.

You can also stop by the reading room at the **Norway-Lithuania Association** (Foreningen Norge-Litauens). This nonprofit organization was chartered to help Scandinavians in Lithuania and Lithuanians who are interested in Scandinavia, but their services are open to anyone. In a comfortable room dozens of books and brochures are for sale. Friendly Mr. Vaseikis offers helpful information, arranges cars and drivers ($1/hour plus gas), and can find you a bed-and-breakfast deal for $15 a night (Monday–Friday 10:00–17:00, at Didžioji g. 13, through the archway by the Norwegian flags, tel. and fax 465 209).

Currency Exchange
Booths everywhere have similar rates. Among others, the Vilniaus Bankas at Gedimino pr. 14 will exchange American Express traveler's checks for a 2.5 percent commission (Monday–Thursday 9:00–12:30 and 14:30–17:00, Friday 9:00–12:30 and 14:30–16:00). The same bank will issue Visa cash advances. 4 litas (Lt) = $1, and 1 litas = 100 centas (c).

Mail and Telephones
The main post office is at Gedimino pr. 7 (Monday–Friday 8:00–20:00, Saturday–Sunday 11:00–19:00). The main telephone office is on Vilniaus g33. (enter from Islandijos g., open 24 hours, tel. 619 614). Here you can make long-distance calls from phones which take wide-grooved tokens that they sell for 20c. If you need to call abroad or for a longer time, buy a card (smallest denomination: 15 Lt) which you can use in the efficient blue Norwegian phones in this office, the train station, and a few other places around town (tear off the corner before you insert the card). Per minute, calls to Russia cost 1.40 Lt; to Latvia or Estonia, 95c; to Europe, 5.8 Lt; and to the U.S., 10.5 Lt. Local calls are currently free from any booth on the street.

Helpful Hints
The **American embassy** is at Akmenu g. 6, slightly west of
the Old Town (tel. 223 031 or 222 729). Though tiny, the
assortment of books, maps, and dictionaries at **Penki
Kontinentai** (Five Continents) is the best in town
(Monday–Friday 10:00–19:00, Stulginskio 5).

Getting Around Vilnius
Vilnius has trolleybuses (with overhead wires) and regular
buses (without wires). Both trolleybuses and buses use named
stops, and people in Vilnius often refer to their location by the
name of the nearest bus stop. The trolleybuses are more convenient, because *Vilnius In Your Pocket* includes a handy map
listing routes and stop names. Tickets, available from kiosks,
cost 20c apiece. The crowding in Vilnius' public transportation
is the worst of any of the cities covered in this book. Bus travel
gets very slow—at every stop, passengers one by one unstick
themselves from their neighbors to let out people even deeper
inside. For the most part, I recommend riding public transportation in Vilnius only if you are with someone you feel
comfortable kissing. Taxis around the center should cost about
5 Lt, never more than 10 Lt, but Vilnius is the hardest Baltic
capital in which to find an honest cabbie.

Sights—Vilnius
▲▲▲**KGB Prison**—After the KGB withdrew from Vilnius,
their former prisoners set up a museum in the building where
they were once held and beaten, and started giving tours to
anyone who would listen. Many Lithuanians were interned
here briefly before being deported to Siberia during the 1940s,
and the part of the building you will see—including the cells,
the padded isolation/torture chamber, appalling photographs
of brutally murdered people, and piles of shredded KGB
documents—is now formally known as the Museum of
Genocide of the People of Lithuania. Ask them to dig up their
English translation of the exhibits. The museum is free, but
despite these people's years of suffering they have very little
budget. Consider dropping a 5-Lt coin in the donation box
(Tuesday–Friday 11:00–13:00 and 14:00–17:00, Saturday and
Sunday 11:00–17:00, Gedimino pr. 40, entrance off Aukų g.,
tel. 622 449).

▲▲**Jewish State Museum**—Its two buildings are a block apart. The **Holocaust Exhibition** is at Pamėnkalnio g. 12, in the green house on the hill. Before World War II, 240,000 Jews lived in Lithuania; 95 percent of them perished during the war. Vilnius, which was 30 percent Jewish in 1914, was for many years the intellectual and cultural center of Eastern European Jewry. The exhibit first documents prewar Jewish life in Vilnius (including blowups of powerful documentary photographs by Roman Vishniac), then its extermination by the Nazis, including one German commandant's chilling daily execution record. Admission is free, but donations are gratefully accepted. The staff will be happy to interpret if they're not busy and can also provide guided tours to Jewish historical sites around Lithuania if you contact them in advance at tel. 620 730 (Monday–Friday 9:00–17:00).

The newly reopened **Exhibition on Jewish Life** is in two rooms on the second floor of Pylimo g. 4. One room shows relics of the city's Great Synagogue, bombed toward the end of World War II and torn down shortly thereafter. The other room is reserved for changing displays. Booklets, postcards, and crafts are on sale (Monday–Friday 11:00–17:00).

Ask the staff at either museum how to get to Paneriai, outside Vilnius, where the Nazis murdered 100,000 people, 70,000 of them Jews.

▲▲**Castle Hill**—Hike up to the top from the square near the cathedral; if it's a nice day, bring a picnic lunch. Buy a ticket (1 Lt, free on Wednesday) and climb up to the roof of Gedimino Tower, at the top of the hill, to see Vilnius spread out before you (and in the distance, to the west, the TV tower where Soviet troops killed 14 unarmed Lithuanians in January 1991). Gedimino Tower (Wednesday–Sunday 11:00–18:00) also houses a small museum.

▲**Lithuanian Art Museum** (Lietuvos Dailės Muziejus)— In the big building in the square where Didžioji g. and Vokiečių g. meet, the second-floor permanent exhibition of Lithuanian art from 1907–1940 is worth a look, especially as a contrast to the cosmopolitan angst of the similar exhibit in Riga. Here the paintings are mostly on rural and domestic themes, and there are some great woodcuts (40c, Tuesday–Sunday 12:00–18:00, free Wednesdays, Didžioji g. 31).

▲**Lithuanian State Museum** (Lietuvos Valstybės
Muziejus)—This large, white, Soviet-modern building along
the north riverbank (past the multi-story Hotel Lietuva)
houses a large collection of Lithuanian religious art and
wood carving, and also an exhibit on Soviet rule in
Lithuania, including the occupation, the deportations, and
the Lithuanian resistance, which unfortunately is inaccessible
unless you read Lithuanian or Russian (40c, Wednesday–
Sunday 11:00–19:00, free Wednesdays).

▲**Lithuanian National Cultural and Historical Museum**
(Lietuvos Nacionalinis Muziejus)—The second-floor exhibition on inter-war independent Lithuania is the most colorful
and thus probably the most interesting to non-Lithuanian
speakers (1 Lt, Wednesday–Sunday 11:00–18:00, October–
April 11:00–17:00, Arsenalo g. 1, in the long, low building at
the northwest base of Castle Hill).

▲**Churches**—Consider visiting the **Vilnius Cathedral**
(Vilniaus Katedra), whose walls and pillars are hung with
dozens of religious paintings (come on Saturday and you
might see a wedding); **St. John's Church** (Šv. Jono) at Pilies
g. and Šv. Jono g.; and the **Gates of Dawn** (Aušros Vartai)
on Aušros Vartų g. (be sure to walk up the long hallway and
the stairs to the chapel in the archway over the street).

▲**Trakai**—This picture-perfect castle is a half-hour from
Vilnius, on an island in the middle of a lake. Buses leave frequently from the Vilnius bus station.

Sleeping in Vilnius
**(4 litas = $1, tel. code: 3702; tel. code within the
Baltics and Russia: 80122)**

Hotels
Hotel Turistas, Vilnius' premier Intourist hotel before
the Lietuva was built, is now under new management.
Eighty clean, standard-issue double rooms with private
bath, TV, and telephone are priced very competitively at
200 Lt–220 Lt, breakfast included. Single occupancy
costs 160 Lt–180 Lt (Ukmėrges g. 14; AmEx and Visa
accepted; tel. 733 106 or 733 102, fax 353 161). The
Turistas' excellent restaurant is downstairs, and the Old
Town is a short walk away.

Hotel Neringas is an acceptable, clean, Soviet-style hotel with a quiet, carpeted lobby. It's central but frankly overpriced. Singles with bath 240 Lt, doubles 300 Lt, breakfast included. Reception on the second floor. Reserve ahead (Gedimino pr. 23, tel. 610 516, fax 614 160).

Zaliasis Tiltas (Green Bridge) is an old, run-down but tolerable Soviet-era hotel with a depressing lobby and a staff that is friendly but doesn't speak much English. Singles with bath 120 Lt–250 Lt, doubles 130 Lt–400 Lt (Gedimino pr. 12, Visa and AmEx accepted, tel. 615 450).

Hotel Astoria, undergoing renovation, will re-open as a four-star hotel. The location can't be beat, the staff are the friendliest around, and the new prices (as yet undisclosed) may be worth the splurge. It's in the center of the Old Town (Didžioji g. 35; AmEx, Visa, MasterCard accepted; tel. 629 914 or 224 020, fax 220 097).

Bed and Breakfasts
Litinterp can house you with a family in the Old Town for 50 Lt–60 Lt single or 100 Lt double, breakfast included (Monday–Friday 9:00–18:00, Saturday 9:00–16:00, Sunday closed, Bernardinų g. 7/2, tel. 223 291 or 223 850, fax 223 559). Also ask them about airport pickup ($10), translators (200 Lt per 10-hour day), long-term apartment rentals (about $300/month), and car rental (175 Lt/day with 200 free kilometers, 125 Lt/day with unlimited mileage for their venerable but popular 1978 Volvo, Visa accepted).

Norway-Lithuania Association (Foreningen Norge-Litauens) will set you up with a family for approximately $15 per person per day (see address under Orientation, above).

Youth Hostels
Lithuanian Youth Hostels (Lietuvos Jaunimo Nakvynės Namai)—Arriving at the train or bus station, you can come straight to the office for advice (Monday–Saturday 8:00–20:00, October–April Monday–Friday 8:00–16:30; Kauno g. 1a, room 407; tel. 262 660, fax 260 631). Head left out of the train station and down Šopeno g., which turns into Kauno g. just after the "Geležinkelio kasos" sign; number 1a is the first Soviet-style building on your right.

They will most likely send you to their main hostel at Filaretų g. 17 (tel. 696 627, fax 220 149), which you can also reach directly by taking bus #34 from outside the train station and to the right to the seventh ("Filaretų") stop. The hostel has 80 beds in two- to six-bed rooms and charges 28 Lt–36 Lt including breakfast. A youth hostel card is required but can be purchased for $7–$9. If this hostel is full they can recommend several other options.

Eating in Vilnius

Lithuania is large enough to have a few truly distinctive culinary concoctions. If you get the chance, try *cepeliniai* (monstrous potato dumplings filled with meat) or *šakotis* (a two-foot-high, spiky cylindrical cake sometimes sold by the layer at cafés).

Turistas—Against all odds, a ground-floor dining room in a vast concrete Soviet-style hotel has been transformed into a warm and serene place to have dinner. Those who've stayed in similar but unreformed provincial hotels in Russia may weep at the sight of this place. The menu is posted at the door, the waiters speak English and smile, there is rarely anything louder than soft piano music, candles shine on every table in the winter, and artfully prepared entrees from a wide-ranging menu average 12 Lt. The still-functioning Soviet hand dryers in the men's room are a metaphor for the whole place (daily 7:30–23:00, Ukmergės g. 14, in the Hotel Turistas; AmEx and Visa accepted).

Medininkai offers filling, satisfying, standard meat-and-potatoes fare under medieval arched ceilings with an English menu. The coat-check routine, the artificially precise prices, and the erratic service are typically Soviet, but entrees (e.g., a chicken cutlet with fries and vegetables) cost only 7 Lt–9 Lt. It's big, so come for dinner when many other restaurants are full up (daily 12:00–23:00, Aušros Vartų g. 8; look for the sign over an archway).

Stikliai, at Stiklių g. 7, was a sensation when it opened in 1987. It used to be called the only restaurant in the Baltics worth eating at. Over the past couple years it has gone exclusive and expensive. The owners have opened a café and a beer bar to compensate. **Stikliai Kavinė** (the café) at Stiklių g. 18 has a Western atmosphere, little tables where a single traveler can sit undisturbed, and for 5 Lt–7 Lt will serve you spaghetti, ice cream, or a mediocre little pizza. There are bigger tables all the way back (Sunday–Friday 9:00–23:00, Saturday 12:00–22:00). **Stikliai Aludė** (the beer bar) has baked potatoes with toppings for 12 Lt–15 Lt as well as soup and some meat and fish entrees for 16 Lt–25 Lt (daily 11:00–24:00, Gaono g. 7 at the corner of Stiklių g.). While both of these places are deservedly popular oases of comfort in Vilnius, the food is only adequate, the all-male wait-staff can be pompous, and some of their popularity comes from their association with the prestigious restaurant.

Ritos Slėptuvė (Rita's Hideout) is along the south bank of the river not far from the KGB prison museum. This dark basement hangout is run by Rita Dapkutė, a Lithuanian-American from Chicago who was the director of the Lithuanian Parliament's Information Bureau during the independence struggle. The menu features spaghetti for 5 Lt–6 Lt and large pizzas for 25 Lt–40 Lt (Goštauto g. 8; enter from a side street called Mečetės g.). You can also order pizza delivery from **Ritos Virtuvė** (Rita's Kitchen) every day from 10:00 until 2:00 in the morning at tel. 626 117; a medium (enough for two-plus people) costs about 40 Lt delivered.

Senas Grafas has nice outdoor tables in a courtyard in summer. Their spaghetti costs 7.20 Lt (Thursday–Tuesday 12:00–23:00, Wednesday 14:00–23:00, Šv. Kazimiero g. 3; coming off Aušros Vartų g. onto Šv. Kazimiero g., look for the "baras" signs).

Literatų Svetainė, across from the cathedral, is a lackluster but reliable choice (daily 12:00–23:00, Gedimino pr. 1).

Geležinis Vilkas is a slightly pretentious and trendy café inside Vilnius' contemporary arts center, right by the art museum and the Hotel Astoria. The arts center is worth a stroll after lunch, which should cost about $5 (daily 11:00–23:00, Vokiečiu g. 2).

Baltu Ainiai, in the old town, is a dark but modern non-alcoholic café which has great poppy-seed cake (Monday–Saturday 10:00–18:00, Savičiaus g. 12).

For picnic fixings, the Vilnius market is just northeast of the train station, in the area bordered by Pylimo g., Bazilijonų g., and Geležinkelio g. For a real supermarket, try Iki, some distance from the center of town at Zirmūnų g. 68

by the "Konstravimo biuras" bus stop (check the map in *Vilnius In Your Pocket*; Monday–Friday 9:00–19:00, Saturday 9:00–18:00).

Near Vilnius: Kaunas

Kaunas was Lithuania's capital between the wars when Vilnius was occupied by Poland. It's cozier, and especially friendlier to people on foot, than Vilnius is. Since its population is 80 percent ethnic Lithuanian as opposed to Vilnius' 50 percent, some claim that Kaunas is the "real Lithuania."

Kaunas is an easy day trip from Vilnius. Minibuses to Kaunas leave roughly hourly from the frontmost platform at Vilnius bus station. Buy your ticket in advance (3.70 Lt—ask for the *mikroautobusas*) but if you show up late you can get it from the driver. The trip takes an hour and 40 minutes. Regular-size buses run to Kaunas every half-hour and are cheaper, but take 2 hours. The train also takes about 2 hours. The Kaunas bus and train stations are a block away from each other but more than a mile from the Old Town.

When you arrive in Kaunas, buy a copy of *Kaunas In Your Pocket* if you didn't get one at the bus station in Vilnius, then get into a taxi and ask to be taken to the Rotušės aikštė (Town Hall square). This should cost about 4 Lt and leave

Kaunas

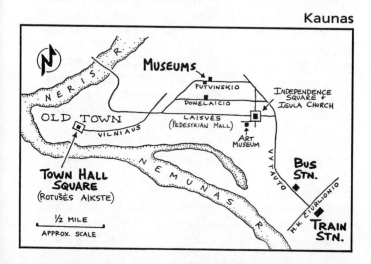

you at the central square of Kaunas's Old Town. From here, you can first explore the Old Town and then walk the approximately 2 km back to the station along Kaunas' grand pedestrian street, called first Vilniaus gatvė and then Laisvės aleja. There are plenty of small cafés along these streets.

One block to the left (north) of Laisvės aleja is Donelaičio g., where you'll find the drab **Military Museum of Vytautas the Great** (Vytauto Didziojo Karo Muziejus), which preserves the airplane in which two Lithuanian-American aviators crashed while trying to make a nonstop New York–Kaunas flight in 1933. Behind this is the **Art Museum** (Dailės Muziejus) in whose newer wing you can listen to music by the Lithuanian composer M. K. Čiurlionis (1875–1911) and then look at paintings in which he tried to present the same structures visually. (Vytautas Landsbergis, the former Lithuanian president, first made his reputation as a Čiurlionis scholar.) Across the street at Putvinskio g. 64 the **Devils' Museum** (Velnių Muziejus) is a collection of hundreds of folk-art devil carvings; the well-known one of Hitler and Stalin divvying up Lithuania is on the second floor. All these museums are open Wednesday through Sunday only. If you have more time you can see the **Ninth Fort** (a notorious Nazi internment camp) or the beautiful **Pazaislis monastery** complex a little outside Kaunas.

Sleeping in Kaunas: A lackluster restaurant scene detracts from the appeal of overnighting in Kaunas, but the Hotel Lietuva at Daukanto g. 21 is central, clean, and reasonably priced: singles with bath cost 160 Lt, doubles with bath 240 Lt–270 Lt, breakfast included, Visa accepted (tel. 205 992; use the prefix 8-27 from Vilnius, 8-0127 from elsewhere in the former Soviet Union, 370 7 from abroad). Lithuanian Youth Hostels puts people up at Prancūzų g. 59 (tel. 748 972, fax 202 761), not far from the stations, for $10.

Transportation Connections—Vilnius

By Train
The Lithuanian Railways (Lietuvos Geležinkeliai) office in the sunken courtyard next to the Hotel Lietuva at Ukmergės g. 20 (tel. 356 225) would be the easiest place to get advance tickets if

Trains Departing Vilnius

#	Destination	Departs	Arrives	2nd class	1st class
6	Moscow	15:23	9:27	80 Lt	129 Lt
88	"	19:44	13:13	"	"
192	St. Petersburg	18:31	10:15	66 Lt	110 Lt
187	Riga	7:30	14:50	39 Lt	70 Lt
621	"	23:21	7:40	"	"
187	Tallinn	16:01	6:49	48 Lt	67 Lt
27	Warsaw*	17:15	6:05	110 Lt	-

*Tickets available only at booking office near Hotel Lietuva. Because this train runs via Grodno, a visa is necessary. See Gateways chapter, Warsaw section.

it weren't for their opening hours (Monday–Friday 10:00–13:00 and 14:00–18:00, Saturday–Sunday 10:00–13:00 and 14:00–16:00). This is the only place where you can get advance tickets to Warsaw or on the Baltic Express to Tallinn. At least one of the staff usually speaks a foreign language.

Advance bookings on trains within the former Soviet Union (except the Baltic Express) can also be made at the reservation office at Šopeno g. 3, down the street from the train station past the bus station—look for the green sign saying "Geležinkelio kasos" (Monday–Saturday 9:00–20:00, Sunday 9:00–17:00).

Tickets for trains leaving in less than 24 hours can be bought only at the station (Geležinkelio stotis). For trains within the former Soviet Union, visit windows 1–6. For trains to Warsaw or for the Baltic Express, visit window 8.

Vilnius, more so than Tallinn or Riga, is a big train junction. Trains arrive from Riga, Kaunas, Kaliningrad, Warsaw, and Berlin on their way to Kiev, Lvov, Moscow, St. Petersburg, and Tallinn. So, for instance, although seven trains a day run from Vilnius to St. Petersburg, virtually all of the tickets to St. Petersburg available in Vilnius will be on the single one that originates in Vilnius. Tickets on trains that originate elsewhere are only available 3 hours before the train's arrival in Vilnius, at the windows in the station labeled "Tranzitniu Traukiniu Bilietu Kasos." I don't recommend trying this unless you're stranded.

The schedule on p. 123 lists only those trains that

originate in Vilnius, plus the connections from Vilnius
to the Tallinn–Kaunas–Šeštokai–Warsaw *Baltic Express*
train.

By Bus
The Vilnius bus station is across the street from the train
station. Look for the "Autobusu stotis" sign. The ticket
windows are in the right half of the building. At the main
windows (numbers 1–11) you can buy tickets for trips
within the old Soviet Union, including Tallinn, Riga, and
destinations within Lithuania. Six buses run to **Riga** every
day at 00:30, 8:00, 9:45, 12:40, 17:10, and 21:45. The ride
takes roughly 5½ hours, and tickets range from 21 Lt–27
Lt. Three of the Riga-bound buses continue on to **Tallinn** (departing Vilnius at 8:00, 9:45, and 21:45, fares from
43 Lt–55 Lt, 12-hour trip). Most can be reserved up to
seven days in advance. An exception is the 12:40 bus to
Riga; tickets are only available 30 minutes prior to
departure.

The international windows (numbered 13–15) sell
tickets to foreign destinations, mostly Poland. These windows are open for advance sales daily 8:00–12:00 and
13:00–17:30, and for same-day tickets 8:00–12:00 and
13:00–23:00. You can try reserving by phone at tel. 635
277. A chart in the windows lists availability (a plus sign
means there are free seats). To **Warsaw**, two fairly comfortable buses leave daily at 10:00 and 14:30, arriving at
Warszawa Zachodnia bus station at 20:00 and 23:45,
respectively. Tickets cost 55 Lt. Monday through Friday,
two overnight buses to Warsaw depart Vilnius at 20:10 and
21:30 (64 Lt, 10½-hour trip). Buses also run from Vilnius
to other cities in Poland.

By Air
Instead of tearing down the old Stalin-era terminal at
Vilnius' airport, or building a new one on a different side of
the runway, they piggybacked a new terminal on top of the
old one. It's a unique creation. Reach the airport on bus #2
(not trolleybus #2), direction: "Aerouostas," from the stop on
the same side of Ukmerge's g. as the Hotel Lietuva; you can
also pick up this bus at several stops closer to the Old Town.

All you need is a regular 20c bus ticket. Taxis from the airport are a rip-off.

You can buy tickets at the airport; at the Lithuanian Airlines (Lietuvos Avialinijos) office at Ukmergės g. 12 (Monday–Friday 9:00–19:00, Saturday 9:00–16:00; round-trip fares to Warsaw start around $100; tel. 753 212); or at Baltic Travel Service in the Old Town (Subačiaus g. 2, tel. 620 757).

TAKING THE TRANS-SIBERIAN RAILWAY EASTWARD

Until recently the Intourist monopoly on eastbound Trans-Siberian tickets meant that travelers in the know took the Trans-Siberian westbound, from Beijing to Moscow. Now the situation has changed, and it is arguably cheaper and easier to get tickets from Moscow to Beijing.

There are three trains per week to Beijing: two Russian trains and one Chinese train. The Russian #20 trains leave Moscow on Friday and Saturday evenings, and arrive the following Friday and Saturday mornings in Beijing, a journey of a little over 6 days. The Chinese #4 train leaves Moscow on Tuesday evenings and arrives in Beijing on the following Monday afternoon, a journey of just over 5½ days. During the summer there is sometimes a third Russian departure on Monday evenings. The train station for all departures to China is Yaroslavskii Vokzal (Ярославский Вокзал) at Metro: Komsomolskaya/Комсомольская; it's the white Art Nouveau station to the right of the Metro building, and the long-distance platforms are on the far side. Arrive at the station an hour before departure.

Routes

Chinese #4 trains from Moscow and Beijing turn south through Mongolia just after they pass Lake Baikal. This route is known as the Trans-Mongolian. Russian #20 trains go around Mongolia to the east, crossing the Russian-Chinese border at Zabaikalsk/Manzhouli and passing through the Chinese city of Harbin. This route is called the Trans-Manchurian. The only train that truly measures up to the name "Trans-Siberian" is the 9-day trip between Moscow and Vladivostok in Russia's Far East.

Visas

You will need a Chinese visa, and if you take the Trans-Mongolian, a Mongolian transit visa as well. Most Chinese consulates issue tourist visas with a minimum of hassle. An exception is the consular office in Moscow (Monday, Wednesday, Friday 9:00–12:00, ul. Druzhby/Дружбы 6,

Metro: Universitet/Университет, tel. 143-1543). They will issue tourist visas only if you show them your ticket to China and your onward ticket from China, or failing that, a "letter of introduction" from your country's embassy. It is better to get your Chinese visa in another country.

Moscow is, however, an excellent place to get your Mongolian transit visa. The Mongolian consular office is at Spasopesovskii/Спасопесовский per. 7/1 (tel. 244-7867), just steps from the Smolenskaya/Смоленская stop on the dark blue metro line. From the Metro exit, go straight through the passage under the modern building, turn right (east) down a small street, and walk one block to a park with a church on the south side and the American ambassador's residence on the east side. The Mongolian complex is on the northwest—look for the pictures of the camels. The consular entrance is through a marked door near the corner of the building (Monday–Friday, 9:00–13:00). If and only if you show them your Chinese visa you will be able to pick up your Mongolian transit visa between 16:30 and 17:00 the same day for $30. One-week processing costs $15. Tourist visas to Mongolia, like those to Russia, still require an official invitation.

From Beijing

Most westbound travelers buy their Beijing–Moscow tickets from Moonsky Star Ltd., popularly known as Monkey Business—a Western-run Trans-Siberian ticket consolidating business. Contact them in Hong Kong at Chung King Mansion, Nathan Road 36-44, E block, fourth floor, flat 6, Kowloon, Hong Kong (tel. 852/723-1376, fax 723-6656, e-mail 100267.2570@compuserve.com). In Beijing, they maintain a branch office in the Qiao Yuan Hotel, new building, room 716, Dongbinhe Rd., Youanmenwei, 100054 Beijing (tel. 86/1/301-2244, ext. 716, fax ext. 444). Work well in advance. They'll help arrange a Russian transit visa, and your ticket will probably include a free night at the Travellers Guest House in Moscow.

The Chinese Train vs. the Russian Train

Travelers on the Chinese train require a $30 Mongolian transit visa, but this is easy to get in Moscow. The Russian

Trans-Siberian Timetable: Moscow to Beijing

The Chinese Train

Day	Time	Station
Tue	19:50	Moscow
Wed	17:35	Perm
Thur	20:09	Novosibirsk
Fri	9:16	Krasnoyarsk
Sat	3:34	Irkutsk
	16:32	Russian-Mongolian border (arr.)
Sun	1:20	Russian-Mongolian border (dep.)
	9:00	Ulaanbaatar
	21:25	Mongolian-Chinese border (arr.)
Mon	1:51	Mongolian-Chinese border (dep.)
	15:33	Beijing

The Russian Train

Day	Time	Station
Fri/Sat	21:25	Moscow
Sat/Sun	19:16	Perm
Sun/Mon	22:11	Novosibirsk
Mon/Tue	10:50	Krasnoyarsk
Tue/Wed	5:16	Irkutsk
Wed/Thur	10:15	Russian-Chinese border (arr.)
	23:13	Russian-Chinese border (dep.)
Thur/Fri	12:09	Harbin
Fri/Sat	6:32	Beijing

Note that all times are local times. For example, the Chinese train arrives in Irkutsk at 7:34 local time, since Irkutsk is 4 hours ahead of Moscow.

train takes about half a day longer than the Chinese train, which can be seen as either an advantage or a disadvantage. The scenery on the two routes is comparable.

The main difference between the two trains is inside the cars. I highly recommend spending the extra money to go first class. Traveling in the Chinese train's first-class, two-person compartments can be a real pleasure: Each compartment has a table, an armchair, and a washroom (including a shower head and occasionally lukewarm water) shared with the adjoining compartment. The Russian train's first-class, two-person compartments are nice too, though plainer. In second class there is less difference: In either case you're in a four-berth compartment of the sort that is great going overnight to St. Petersburg or Tallinn, gets awfully cramped after 5 days, but can be a lot of fun if you have good company. The Chinese train also has some first-class four-berth compartments, which should be your last choice as they combine the high price of first class with the claustrophobia of having three companions.

The Chinese train has Chinese conductors and furnishings, so you may feel as if you've stepped into China already at the Moscow railway station. During the last two days of a trip on the Russian train, you may feel like you're stuck in a little capsule of Russianness that is persisting into China. This is not true in the restaurant car, which changes at each border.

Food

The food in the restaurant car is usually edible, but one such dining experience per day is enough. Before you go, visit one or more of the most well-stocked Western supermarkets in Moscow and load up with enough to feed yourself breakfast plus one meal a day. Some suggestions: bottled water, juice, bread and fruit for the first few days, crisp bread, peanut butter, jelly, tuna fish, chocolate, and yogurt (the kind that needs no refrigeration). Also bring instant soup, tea, and anything else that you just add hot water to, as a samovar in each car is kept boiling most of the time.

Books

The best guidebook to the Trans-Siberian is Bryn Thomas' *Trans-Siberian Handbook*. If you read German, Doris Knop's *Reisen mit der Trans-Sib* is worthwhile for its carefully drawn diagrams. Bring a shorter novel than *War and Peace*—on the trip you'll probably be too busy meeting your fellow travelers and buying berries from grandmothers at whistle-stop stations in Siberia to read anything really heavy.

Buying Tickets for the Trans-Siberian

From Moscow's Central Railway Agency
If you have friends in Moscow or enough time there yourself, this is the cheapest way to go. Take the Metro to

Komsomolskaya/Комсомольская, go out to the street, find
Yaroslavskii Vokzal (the white, Art Nouveau station), and
then look for the nine-floor, brown apartment building
next to it at Krasnoprudnaya/Краснопрудная ul. 1. On the
first floor of this building, on the side facing the station, is
the branch of the Central Railway Agency where most people buy their Trans-Siberian tickets. You can recognize it
by the sign saying Железнодорожные Кассы over the door.
Inside you'll see many people from China and Mongolia.
Head first to any of windows 5–8. Prepare a piece of paper
listing the number of people traveling, your name, nationality, passport number, destination, desired departure date,
and desired class. The women at the ticket counters usually
speak Russian only, but will probably understand your
request even if it's written in Latin letters. If seats are
available, they will produce a piece of paper which you
must take to window 9 or 10, where you pay, in cash rubles
only. With your receipt, you return to the initial window
to pick up your ticket. Window 4 is for information, and
window 3 is the "administrator" (the office boss).

You don't have to come to the office in person to buy
tickets. Someone else can do it for you if they come prepared
with the cash and your full name, nationality, and passport
number, all of which will be listed on your ticket.

The prices in 1996 are roughly $400 per person in a
first-class, two-berth compartment and $300 in a second-
class, four-berth compartment.

Demand varies considerably. Tickets to China go on
sale at this office 30 days in advance. At some times of the
year very few people are traveling, there are no lines at the
office, seats are available even just a few days in advance,
and you'll have your tickets in a matter of minutes. At
other times—mainly from May to September, and during
school vacations from mid-January to mid-February—
bookings are heavy, lines at the office are not long but
move very slowly, and you need to come 2 or 3 weeks in
advance to get seats, or at least the seats you want. The
Chinese train tends to have more space than the Russian
trains, because getting a Mongolian transit visa is a disin-
centive to many people.

From the Travellers Guest House in Moscow

This is the next best alternative. In 1995 they charged roughly $355 per person in second class and $450 in two-berth, first class, whether it's on the Chinese or the Russian train. They also can sell you tickets which allow you to stop in Irkutsk and/or Mongolia along the way, including accommodations and the more expensive programs tours and meals as well. From April to October, they can also get you train tickets from Moscow to Urumchi in northwestern China, along the recently opened rail line through Kazakhstan. Contact them in Moscow at tel. 971-4059, fax 280-7686, e-mail tgh@glas.apc.org.

From St. Petersburg International Hostel's American Office

You can also book tickets or tours through the St. Petersburg International Hostel's American office at 409 N. Pacific Coast Highway, Bldg. #106, Suite 390, Redondo Beach, CA 90277. For specifics, contact them at tel. 310/618-2014 or fax 618-1140.

From Finnish Railways (VR)

This is an option if you can pass through Helsinki to pick them up. There are some drawbacks (second-class Russian train only, reconfirmation in Moscow). Contact VR in the Helsinki train station or at 358/0/707-3411, fax 358/0/707-4240.

APPENDIX

Baltic Timeline

1200–1300: German merchants and clerics attempt respectively to colonize the Baltic states and Christianize their native populations. A German class of land-owning nobles emerges in Estonia and Latvia. Lithuania resists.

1386: Preferring the Poles to the Germans, the Prince of Lithuania marries the Princess of Poland and unites the two countries. Catholicism becomes the state religion.

1520s: The Reformation reaches Estonia and Latvia.

1629: Sweden acquires most of Estonia and Latvia.

1700–1721: Russia wins Estonia and Latvia from Sweden in the Great Northern War.

1795: Lithuania becomes part of the Russian Empire in the third partition of Poland.

1850–1890: Independence movements start to roll. Ethnic and national consciousness grows in the Baltics.

1918–1921: The Baltics gain independence in the wake of the Russian Revolution and the First World War, but have to fight both the Germans and the Red Army for it. Ethnic Germans start leaving Estonia and Latvia.

1939: The secret Molotov-Ribbentrop pact between Hitler's Germany and Stalin's Russia declares the Baltic states part of Russia's sphere of influence.

1940–1945: The Baltics become a political football between Russia and Germany. Net result: Mass deportations of Balts to Siberia and of Jews to the Nazi concentration camps, and the Soviet annexation of all three Baltic states.

1945–1989: Sovietization. Ethnic Russians move into the Baltics to take military and civilian jobs.

1989–1991: Under *glasnost*, a mass movement for an end

to Soviet occupation and the restoration of independence gains steam. Lithuania declares independence first; Moscow's armed reprisals leave 14 dead in Vilnius.

August 1991: World recognition of Baltic independence comes in the wake of the failed coup in Moscow.

Russian Timeline

800s: Spurred by Viking trade along Russia's rivers, states form around the cities of Novgorod and Kiev. ("Russia" comes from a Viking word.)

988: Kiev converts to Christianity and becomes part of the Eastern Orthodox world.

1224–1242: The Mongol hordes invade Russia, conquer, and exact tribute. Russia, however, succeeds where the Baltics failed: at keeping the Germans out.

1465–1557: The Russian czars consolidate power in Moscow, drive away the Mongols, and form a unified Russian state.

1613: Foundation of the Romanov dynasty, which lasts until 1917.

1703: Czar Peter the Great founds St. Petersburg as Russia's "window on the West." Major phase of southward and eastward Russian expansion under Peter and his successor Catherine.

1812: Napoleon burns Moscow, but loses an army on the way home.

1855–1861: Russia loses Crimean War and decides to modernize, including freeing the serfs.

1905: Russia loses a war with the Japanese, contributing to a failed revolution later glorified by the Communists as a manifestation of worker's consciousness.

1917: In March, the czar is ousted by a Provisional Government led by Aleksandr Kerensky.

1917:	In November, the Provisional Government is ousted by the Bolsheviks (Communists), led by Lenin.
1924–1939:	Stalin purges the government and the army, and forced collectivization causes famine and tens of millions of deaths in Ukraine.
1939–1945:	World War II. Russia loses another 20 million to the Germans, but winds up with control over a sizable chunk of Eastern Europe.
1945–1962:	Peak of the Cold War. Russia acquires the atom bomb, and launches the first satellite and the first manned space mission.
1970s:	The "time of stagnation" under Leonid Brezhnev. The failure of the Communist economy becomes more and more apparent.
1985:	Mikhail Gorbachev comes to power and declares the beginning of *glasnost* (openness) and *perestroika* (restructuring).
1991:	Reactionaries try to topple Gorbachev. They fail to keep power, but so does Gorbachev. Boris Yeltsin takes control of the government and starts reforms.
1993:	Reactionaries try to topple Yeltsin. They fail to gain power, but Yeltsin is weakened.
1995:	Boris Yeltsin hangs on to power, while grumbling from the ultra-nationalist right wing grows.
1996:	Stay tuned . . .

Telephone Directory

From Outside Russia and the Baltics
Country Codes: Estonia 372, Latvia 371, Lithuania 370, Russia 7.
City Codes: Tallinn, Riga, and Vilnius are each 2. Moscow 095, St. Petersburg 812.

Within Russia and the Baltics
All calls are dialed as if the entire area were still part of the U.S.S.R. This means you dial 8 for long distance, then the

old Soviet city code (Moscow 095, St. Petersburg 812, Tallinn 0142, Riga 0132, Vilnius 0122), then the local number. To make international calls from the Baltics and Russia, you dial 8, wait for a tone, and then dial 10 followed by the country code, area code, and local number.

AT&T USA Direct Service

In...	Dial...
Lithuania	8-(wait for tone)-196
Latvia	700-7007
Estonia	810-800-1001
Moscow*	155-5042

*From other Russian cities, you can reach Moscow USA Direct by dialing 8-095-155-5042, but you'll have to pay for the long-distance call to Moscow.

Public Holidays
Russia: Jan. 1 (New Year's), Jan. 7 (Christmas), March 8 (Women's Day), May 1, May 9 (Victory Day), June 12 (Independence Day), Dec. 31 (New Year's Eve).

Estonia: Jan. 1 (New Year's), Feb. 24 (Independence Day), Good Friday, May 1, June 23 (Victory Day), June 24 (Midsummer), Nov. 16 (Rebirth Day), Dec. 25-26 (Christmas).

Latvia: Jan. 1 (New Year's), Good Friday, Easter, May 1, June 23-24 (Midsummer), Nov. 18 (Independence Day), Dec. 25-26 (Christmas), Dec. 31 (New Year's Eve).

Lithuania: Jan. 1 (New Year's), Feb. 16 (Independence Day), Easter (Sunday and Monday), May 1, July 6 (Statehood Day), Nov. 1 (All Saints), Dec. 25-26 (Christmas).

Learning Cyrillic

This page and the next contain practical language information that you should tear out and keep in your pocket for those times when you are separated from your guidebook.

Russia uses the Cyrillic alphabet. If you spend 15 minutes learning it, you'll be able to read maps, street signs, food labels, subway directions, train schedules, menus, inscriptions, names of famous people, and Russian graffiti. Ignore Cyrillic, and you'll be completely unable to get around on public transportation, unable even to write the name of a destination for a taxi driver or train-ticket seller, unable to read a street sign, and totally reliant on English-speaking (hard-cash-hungry) Russians. Tape this rip-out cheat sheet to the inside of your glasses. Chant it before going to sleep. Do whatever you need to do—just learn it. Also, some people don't realize that you can read Cyrillic words out loud. When you say Nevsky Prospekt, you're also saying Невский Проспект.

Cyrillic	English spelling	*Sounds like:*	Cyrillic	English spelling	*Sounds like:*
А а	a	Ra*ch*maninoff	Т т	t	Turgenev
Б б	b	*B*aryshnikov	У у	u	*U*stinov
В в	v	Uncle *V*anya	Ф ф	f	*F*runze
Г г	g	*G*ogol	Х х	kh	as in the
Д д	d	*D*ostoevskii			Scottish lo*ch*
Е е	e	*Y*eltsin	Ц ц	ts	*Ts*arevich
Ё ё	yo	*Y*ossarian	Ч ч	ch	T*ch*aikovsky
Ж ж	zh	Bre*zh*nev	Ш ш	sh	Pu*sh*kin
З з	z	*Z*amiatin	Щ щ	shch	Khru*shch*ev
И и	i	*I*zvestiya	Ъ ъ	—	"hard sign"
Й й	i	Tolsto*y*			(ignore it)
К к	k	*C*atherine	Ы ы	y	Solzhenits*y*n
Л л	l	*L*enin	Ь ь	—	"soft sign"
М м	m	*M*olotov			(ignore it)
Н н	n	*N*abokov	Э э	e	*E*thelr*e*d the
О о	o	*O*blomov			Unr*ea*dy
П п	p	*P*asternak			
Р р	r	*R*asputi	Ю ю	yu	*Yu*goslavia
С с	s	*S*uvorov	Я я	ya	*Ya*lta

Buying Train Tickets

Please help me to buy the following tickets:
Пожалуйста; помагите мене купить эти билеты:

Destination/До станции _____
Month/Месяц: _____ Date/Число: _____
Train number/Поезд Nr _____
Departure time/Отправление в _____

Number of passengers/Количество человек: _____
Class/Тип: 2-berth/СВ
4-berth/купейный
Sitting place/Сиденный

Surname(s)/Фамипия: _____
Citizenship/Гражданство: _____

Нет мест.
There are no seats available.

Мест ест; но в другом классе.
There are seats, but only in a different class.

Здесь не продаём.
We don't sell these tickets at this window.

Basic Survival Phrases

In the following list, pronounce *a* as in car, *e* as in bet, *i* as in spaghetti, *o* as in more, *u* as in tune. Ä, ö, and ü in Estonian have the same sounds as umlauts in German (*ä* is like the English *a* in cat; for *ö* and *ü*, try to say "e" with your lips rounded).

English	Estonian	Latvian	Lithuanian	Russian
yes	ya	yä	taip	da
no	ei	nē	ne	nyet
hello	tere	labdien	laba diena	zdrastvuytye
goodbye	head aega	visugaishu	viso gero	do svidanya
Please	palun	ludzu	prashom	pazhalsta
thank you	tänan	paldies	achu	spasiba
excuse me	vabandage	atvainoyiet	atsiprashau	izvinitye
one	üks	viens	vienas	adin
two	kaks	divs	du	dva
three	kolm	tris	tris	tri
Where is...?	Kus on...?	Kur ir...?	Kur...?	Gdye...?
How much?	Kui palyu maksab?	Tsik maksā?	Kiek kainuoya?	Skolka stoyit?
I don't understand	Ma ei sa aru	Es nesaprotu	Ash nesuprantu	Nye ponil
Do you speak English?	Kas tele räägite inglise keelt?	Vai jūs runājet-angliski?	Ar kalbates anglishkai?	Vi gavaritye pa angliski?

Cyrillic	English	Sounds like:	Cyrillic	English	Sounds like:
А а	a	Rachmaninoff	Р р	r	Rasputin
Б б	b	Baryshnikov	С с	s	Suvorov
В в	v	Uncle Vanya	Т т	t	Turgenev
Г г	g	Gogol	У у	u	Ustinov
Д п	d	Dostoevskii	Ф ф	f	Frunze
Е е	e	Yeltsin	Х х	kh	as in the Scottish loch
Ё ё	yo	Yossarian	Ц ц	ts	Tsarevich
Ж ж	zh	Brezhnev	Ч ч	ch	Tchaikovsky
З з	z	Zamiatin	Ш ш	sh	Pushkin
И и	i	Izvestiya	Щ щ	shch	Khrushchev
Й й	i	Tolstoy	Ъ ъ	-	"hard sign" (ignore it)
К к	k	Catherine	Н ы	y	Solzhenitsyn
Л п	l	Lenin	Ь ь	-	"soft sign" (ignore it)
М м	m	Molotov	Э э	e	Ethelred the Unready
Н н	n	Nabokov	Ю ю	yu	Yugo
О о	o	Oblomov	Я я	ya	Yalta
П п	p	Pasternak			

INDEX

Other Books from John Muir Publications

Travel Books by Rick Steves

Asia Through the Back Door, $17.95

Europe 101: History and Art for the Traveler, $17.95

Mona Winks: Self-Guided Tours of Europe's Top Museums, $18.95

Rick Steves' Baltics & Russia, $9.95

Rick Steves' Europe, $17.95

Rick Steves' France, Belgium & the Netherlands, $13.95

Rick Steves' Germany, Austria & Switzerland, $13.95

Rick Steves' Great Britain, $13.95

Rick Steves' Italy, $13.95

Rick Steves' Scandinavia, $13.95

Rick Steves' Spain & Portugal, $13.95

Rick Steves' Europe Through the Back Door, $18.95

Rick Steves' French Phrase Book, $4.95

Rick Steves' German Phrase Book, $4.95

Rick Steves' Italian Phrase Book, $4.95

Rick Steves' Spanish & Portuguese Phrase Book, $5.95

Rick Steves' French/German/Italian Phrase Book, $6.95

For Birding Enthusiasts

The Birder's Guide to Bed and Breakfasts: U.S. and Canada, $17.95

The Visitor's Guide to the Birds of the Central National Parks: U.S. and Canada, $15.95

The Visitor's Guide to the Birds of the Eastern National Parks: U.S. and Canada, $15.95

The Visitor's Guide to the Birds of the Rocky Mountain National Parks: U.S. and Canada, $15.95

A Natural Destination Series

Belize: A Natural Destination, $16.95

Costa Rica: A Natural Destination, $17.95

Guatemala: A Natural Destination, $16.95

Unique Travel Series

Each is 112 pages and $10.95 paper, except Georgia.

Unique Arizona
Unique California
Unique Colorado
Unique Florida
Unique Georgia ($11.95)
Unique New England
Unique New Mexico
Unique Texas
Unique Washington

2 to 22 Days Itinerary Planners

2 to 22 Days in the American Southwest, $11.95

2 to 22 Days in Asia, $10.95

2 to 22 Days in Australia, $11.95

2 to 22 Days in California, $11.95

2 to 22 Days in Eastern Canada, $11.95

2 to 22 Days in Florida, $11.95

2 to 22 Days Around the Great Lakes, $11.95

2 to 22 Days in Hawaii, $11.95

2 to 22 Days in New England, $11.95

2 to 22 Days in New Zealand, $11.95

2 to 22 Days in the Pacific Northwest, $11.95

2 to 22 Days in the Rockies, $11.95

2 to 22 Days in Texas, $11.95

2 to 22 Days in Thailand, $10.95

Other Terrific Travel Titles

The 100 Best Small Art Towns in America, $12.95

The Big Book of Adventure Travel, $17.95

California Public Gardens, $16.95

Indian America: A Traveler's Companion, $18.95

The People's Guide to Mexico, $19.95

Ranch Vacations: The Complete Guide to Guest and Resort, Fly-Fishing, and Cross-Country Skiing Ranches, $19.95

Understanding Europeans, $14.95

Undiscovered Islands of the Caribbean, $16.95

Watch It Made in the U.S.A.: A Visitor's Guide to the Companies that Make Your Favorite Products, $16.95

Ordering Information

Please check your local bookstore for our books, or call 1-800-888-7504 to order direct and to receive a complete catalog. A shipping charge will be added to your order total.

Send all inquiries to:
John Muir Publications
P.O. Box 613
Santa Fe, NM 87504